RIDERS OF THE
WINDS

RIDERS of the WINDS

by EDWARD SHENTON

with drawings by the author

MACRAE ✠ SMITH ✠ COMPANY

PHILADELPHIA

To
Jimmy,
Jack and Eddie,
who all should be
flying about the same
time.

CONTENTS

CONTENTS

8   **CONTENTS**

I L L U S T R A T I O N S

TWO MEN COME DOWN IN THE SEA

HARRY HAWKER AND LIEUTENANT-COMMANDER KENNETH MACKENZIE-GRIEVE IN THE "ATLANTIC"

From St. John's, Newfoundland, to forced landing in the Atlantic Ocean . . . Distance approximately 1000 miles . . . Flying time 11 hours . . . May 18, 1919.

MIDWAY in the Atlantic Ocean, a small tramp steamer plowed through a tumultuous sea. A slight rain fell, and half a gale streaked the long waves with foam and shrilled in the rigging. It was a bleak gray day, typical of northern waters, and the wandering little freighter was the only vessel in sight on the lead-colored waste of the sea. The look-out stood, head bent to the wind, in the bows, and the officer on the bridge stared into the hazy distance and thought of the hot coffee waiting at the end of his watch. The waves thudded under the forefoot, the wind wailed and sighed, the thousand and one noises of a ship under way, came to the ears of the mate, so familiar that he scarcely was conscious of them.

Suddenly there was a new sound amid the monotonous symphony of wind and water and straining hull. The mate's head jerked up in astonishment. He saw the lookout, alert, poised, perplexedly gaping to locate the strange roaring. It seemed to come from all directions; ahead, behind, out of the dull sky above. The mate turned and peered into the misty heavens. His jaw dropped and an expression of bewildered unbelief swept across his face. Dipping sharply out of the heavy clouds was a curious kind of kite; no, an extraordinary bird! No, by all the lockers of Davy Jones—an airplane. It came whirling down at them, its motor thundering,—but with an irregular choking instead of the usual steady roar—the propeller making a disk of spinning silver, the great wings magnified by the uncertain visibility. The mate hung onto the swaying bridge-rail, astounded.

The sudden appearance of a whale, the tall ghostly island of an iceberg, a derelict-ship like a floating reef, even the Flying Dutchman, scudding with royals and skysails set, would not have surprised this hardened seaman for more than a moment. But an airplane, in mid-Atlantic —— Great shades of Jonah! He gasped and sent a hasty word to the Captain. Captain Duhn, master of the tramp steamer *Mary* of Copenhagen, came plunging onto the bridge. By this time the airplane was close to the ship. They could see two men in the narrow fuselage. The plane circled the ship twice while the aviators made frantic signals which added to the mystification of the officers of the *Mary.*

" It's beyond me," said the mate. " They want something, or they want to tell us something, or . . . Suppose they're lost, Cap'n? "

" Lost? " said Captain Duhn. " Then they're a long way lost, I'd say. Hey, look! Merciful heavens! . . ."

The plane had been turned in the same direction the steamer was traveling. Now, to the amazement of the two officers and of the entire deck-crew of the *Mary* gathered on the forecastle head, the airplane was gliding steadily down to the sea. A chorus of shouts blew back on the wind.

" Say! Look! They're fallin' ! "

" She's gonna plunge! "

" There she goes! "

" There she . . . She's down! "

The plane struck about a mile beyond the steamer. A wall of white water hid it from view, but when the spray settled they

could see it, badly torn but still afloat, with the two aviators scrambling up from the submerged cockpit.

"Get a boat ready, Mr. Mate," said Captain Duhn grimly. "If that crazy flying-machine stays afloat for ten minutes we'll have 'em off safe an' sound."

The difficult launching was accomplished and twenty minutes later the two flyers scrambled up the swaying ladder to greet the Captain.

In this dramatic fashion ended the first attempt to fly across the Atlantic. The two men were Harry Hawker, a young Australian pilot, and Lt. Commander Kenneth Mackenzie-Grieve of the British Royal Navy, navigator. Both had served with honors in the war that had just ended, and both were still restless and eager for adventure.

The reason for the flight was an attempt to win the prize of £10,000 offered in 1913 by the *Daily Mail* to the crew of the first airplane to fly the Atlantic. Their plane had been built by the Sopwith Aviation Company especially for the effort and after a thorough testing was transported to St. Johns, Newfoundland, in March of 1918, assembled, flown a few times and then loaded with gas and oil, ready to hop off at the first sign of good weather. Their preparations were as complete as possible. The biplane had a detachable undercarriage, to be dropped as soon as the machine had taken the air. A section of the fuselage could be loosened and used as a boat; the flying-suits of the two men had air-bags which would keep them afloat: on board the plane were signal lights, paddles, rations and a small wireless set.

They took off close to six o'clock in the afternoon of May 18th, dropped the undercarriage and headed on their long journey. Conditions were none too favorable. Almost at once they encountered rain, fog and a beam-wind that increased their drift and wasted power. Still, none of these were serious handicaps and they forged ahead. Five hours out Hawker noticed the temperature gauge of the motor rising steadily. This *was* serious. The engine began overheating. There was very little they could do. Hawker dived the plane hoping to force out whatever was obstructing the water-circulation. All night they flew, buffeted by storm after storm, driven out of their course, watching with blood-shot eyes the gradual ascent of the mercury in the thermometer, listening to the engine for some unexpected note in its deep roar. It took cool courage, a clear mind and firm nerves, but they never lost hope. By morning the trouble was so far advanced that they knew a forced landing was a matter of only a short time.

" Find a ship, what? " Hawker shouted.

THE AIRPLANE WAS DESCENDING INTO THE SEA

His companion looked up, grinned and swept his hand in a circle marking the dim horizon.

" Absolutely," said Mackenzie-Grieve.

Five thousand feet below them the torn surface of the Atlantic lay empty from horizon to horizon. Hawker sent the Sopwith zigzagging through the heavens while both men scanned with tense interest the desolate sea. Their lives depended upon the sighting of a vessel, and they knew that the chances against it were about a thousand to one. An hour passed, another. Their eyes ached with the effort of trying to see through the fog and rain. Then Hawker shouted in triumph. Hull down to the east was a dark object, a toy-ship, with a fine thread of smoke rising from its single funnel. He banked over, throttled the hot motor and headed for the steamer. No taking chances now. A long steady descent carried them to the craft. Twice they circled it to make certain of being seen and then crashed the biplane into the turbulent ocean.

There was no wireless on the *Mary* and six days passed before they sighted the Lloyd signal station on the Butt of Lewis and news of the rescue was flashed to London. They had been given up for lost and when the word of their safety came, England went wild with excitement and joy. The arrival of Hawker and Grieve began a triumphal reception almost unequalled. Although they had failed, there was about the expedition such an air of resourceful courage, such an element of dramatic good fortune, that the outcome was more thrilling, probably, than if it had been successful. They were received and decorated by the King, fêted by nobility and idolized by the people. And as though their good star was reluctant to leave them, the battered remains of the abandoned airplane was found by an American steamer, five days later, still afloat, and brought ashore, as a record of hardihood in the face of disaster.

PILGRIMS OF THE AIR

LT. COMMANDER A. C. READ AND CREW OF THE "NC–4"

From Far Rockaway, L. I., to Plymouth, England . . . Distance 3925 miles . . . Flying time approximately 70 hours . . . May 8–31, 1919.

THE end of the war found hundreds of young men dreaming of glory in the air. Among the high white clouds massed over Kelly Field, they had been learning to fly in the slow, sturdy Jennys. They spun and looped and did figure-eights and thought of Richthofen in a bright red Fokker leading his Circus in a wild dive out of the sun upon some unsuspecting dawn patrol.

The very words "dawn patrol" held something mysterious and beautiful and tragic. These boys, starting the day's vigorous training in the gray light of early morning, imagined themselves strapped in a fast, erratic Camel fighting plane, with two thick black machine guns lying along the round cowling, watching the slow ticking propeller and awaiting the signal that would send them hurtling into the cold upper air to death or glory. Among this brood of the eagle, just learning the dangers of a flat-spin and a cross-wind landing, were young men whose names were later to be flung to the stars.

While these fledgling pilots were dreaming of dog-fights and bombing raids and trench-straffing, other aviators, just as young, but with more experience, boys from France and England were actually fighting. Ten thousand feet above the war-torn earth they were diving, whirling, twisting; motors wide open, howling to silence the high wailing of the wind; wires and struts strained to the limit and shrieking like insane birds; machine guns splitting glints of tracer bullets and the invisible lead.

But the war was over!

There was no longer a chance for adventures fighting among the clouds; opportunity beckoned in new directions. Space was to be conquered, and space when it lay above water increased the dare. Peace opened more ways to fame and the dangers were not lessened. Hawker and Grieve were the first to accept the challenge. They failed, but won a lasting place among the lists of the bold. Alcock and Brown were rushing the final tests for their attempt to span the Atlantic and from all corners of the world young pilots were watching with envy, longing for a chance to risk their lives.

These were individual exploits, desperate gambles with machines of uncertain capacity; with only one chance in fifty of success. These pioneers flung their rebuilt war-bombers recklessly into the windy skies to live or die as fortune directed.

While everyone was watching, fascinated, these first valiant flights; slowly, carefully, efficiently, an argosy of the air was being prepared for launching. Under the direction of the Navy Department, Curtiss was building four giant flying-boats for a flight from the United States to England. This was no hit-or-miss striving for prizes or fame. It was a development of the war. Can we build craft capable of cruising over the sea; craft of such dependability that the chance of failure will be reduced to a minimum? What is the safest and surest route to Europe for planes and crews? What kind of plane is best suited to all the conditions of such a venture? The Navy heads called Glenn Curtiss into consultation. Although the war had ended, the plans begun almost two years before were pushed to completion.

The attention of everyone interested in aviation was fixed upon

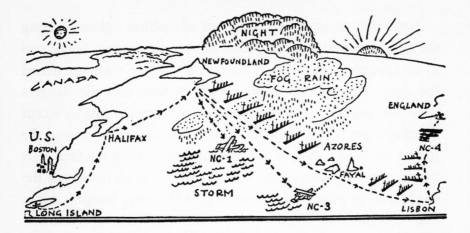

these planes.   The hulls, shaped like immense torpedoes were
44 ½ feet in length with 10 foot beam, larger than the average
yacht, and designed to survive any storm less than a hurricane.
The lower wings swept out from either side of the hull; the
huge upper wing measured 126 feet and the rudders and elevators were built like a gigantic box-kite and extended far in the
rear.   Power to lift the planes came from four four-hundred
horse power Liberty motors.   The two center motors were set in
line, the forward motor turned a propeller which pulled; the
propeller of the rear motor pushed.   The nacelles of the port
and starboard motors were suspended between the wings and
were tractors; that is, operating propellers that pulled the ship
ahead.   In the bow cockpit the commander and navigator rode;
amidship two pilots sat side by side before dual control systems;
aft was the cockpit for engineer and radio operator who had a
complete sending and receiving set.   Fuel tanks were built in
the hull and passage was easily made from one section to another.

When loaded, and with the crew aboard, these ships weighed twelve and one-half tons each.

The workmanship on the four planes was the most skillful that could be obtained. Special navigation instruments were designed for the flight. Master mechanics tuned the motors until the rhythm of their twelve cylinders was like the steady beat of great drums. The hulls had been designed by expert builders of racing boats so they would plane quickly and easily with the least possible friction or air suction, enabling the NC's to rise from the water without too much strain. The personnel of the crews was the pick of the Navy Flying Corps. There was no question of time, money or trouble; everything was the best. When the four ships were complete there were no planes in the world to compare with them. Their commanders were the proudest men in the Navy; not a member of their crews would have changed places with the President of the United States.

In the lengthening April days, the finishing touches were put upon the four craft, and final plans for the flight completed with the same care that marked the work on the planes. No detail was omitted; no resource of the Navy unemployed. The start was to be from Far Rockaway, L. I., where the flying-boats were built; and the first flight ended at Trepassey Bay, Newfoundland, 1100 air-miles away. From there the course lay over the Atlantic to the Azores; approximately 1200 miles, then a shorter hop of 800 miles to Lisbon, Portugal, and final span of 775 miles to Plymouth, England. Sixty destroyers at regularly designated points, guarded the oversea sections, ready to furnish guidance to the planes, or assistance in case of trouble. The position of each of these lean grayhounds of the sea was indicated on the charts of the flyers. Every possible chance of error was eliminated.

Commander John H. Towers, leader of the expedition, gazing at the four great craft, resting on skids before the hangars, visioned them swooping down in formation out of the clear evening sky into the quiet waters of Horta harbor. It was a dream to stir the blood of any man. Surely Columbus, John Cabot, or Magellan were no more daring pioneers than these men, who " in line with duty " were to follow the unknown pathless skies to new adventures. It was just that the leader should stand, quiet and apart sometimes, anticipating, not the danger, but the proud responsibility of his position. There they were, four creations of steel, wood, aluminum and canvas; something new and strange under the sun; the answer to one of man's oldest longings. To fly! To rise from slow plodding of the earth for the hazardous crossing of the seas. To add a new dimension; conquer the last stronghold of Nature; assail the invisible keep of the heavens; to ride, defiantly, the turbulent winds, leap the frail mountains of the clouds; enter the shoreless rivers of the rain; plunge into the sightless twilight of the fog. Here was a region worthy of man's desires, of his best efforts.

But the dreams of man were always sport for the Gods.

Misfortunes began. A storm smashed the wings of the NC-1. The NC-2 was put out of commission and its wings put on the NC-1. The crew of the abandoned ship were heart-broken. One of the best mechanics in the crews had his hand severed from his arm by the unexpected, vicious whirl of a propeller. It was a shocking accident.

" It's not the loss of the hand I mind so much," he said grimly, " it's losing out on the flight." Such was the spirit of the men of the NC's.

That was not the end of the bad luck. A week later the crews were aroused from sleep by a wild uproar. Just as they were, in pajamas, they rushed out of their quarters. Streamers of orange flame sprang from the hangar sheltering the NC-3 and NC-1. The sight sent their hearts in a sickening leap into their throats. Was this to be the funeral pyre of their hopes? Not if they could help it. Recklessly they plunged into the burning hangar. At the expense of seared skins, singed hair and lashes, they rescued the NC-3, but the flames had badly damaged the NC-1. The crew of the battered ship stared in dismay at the warped and blackened wings; then they began repairs. In two weeks the three planes were ready.

Down the greased ways they slid into the water of the Sound. Slowly they taxied into position. The roar of the motors deepened suddenly. From the shore, the disconsolate crew of the NC-2, and Special Mechanic Howard, his arm still bandaged, waved a last farewell. Into the light morning wind the three planes headed, trailing long feathery wakes of white water. Suddenly there was space showing under the dark hulls. Heading east, they gained altitude gradually, lost form in the sun-haze; the thin lines of their wings could no longer be seen, only the dark formless spot of the hulls. Then they had vanished.

The NC-1 and NC-3 reached Trepassey Bay without incident,

but the NC-4 was forced to come down off Cape Cod and taxi to the Naval Station at Chatham for repairs to one of the motors. These were made and they joined their companions in the Newfoundland Harbor.

While this first flight had been almost as far as the next leg to the Azores, still it did not present many dangers or any difficult problems of navigation. They had rarely been out of touch with the land and most of the distance the shore line could be dimly seen away to the left.

Commanders and crews were delighted with the manner in which the great planes had handled. Confidently they prepared for the next hop. They planned to leave as closely as possible to the time of the full moon in order to have its light during the hours of night flying. On the afternoon of May 16th the three flying-boats taxied into position, heading down the long narrow harbor. From the bow cockpit of the NC-3, Flight-Commander Towers waved the signal. The rising thunder of the motors reverberated from the hills overlooking the harbor. Intently the pilots held the control-wheels well forward, helping to lift the heavy hulls onto the " step," that abrupt cut in the bottom which frees a hydroplane hull from water and air suction. The harbor was none too smooth and the snub noses of the three boats beat the choppy sea into a fountain of spray. Now the pilots were bringing the wheels back, lifting the elevators at the rear. The NC-3 porpoised for a moment, skimming the wave crests, then it was up, followed by the other two.

Less than five hundred years before another argosy of three ships had set out from the far side of the world, sailing west into

the unknown. Perhaps, these modern explorers of the air remembered for a moment the *Santa Maria,* the *Nina* and *Pinta,*
as they rose above the harbor and adjusted their course for the
goal of the Azores. Probably they were much too busy. On
the *Santa Maria,* Columbus and his sailors had endless weeks to
plan, to maneuver their clumsy vessel, to set their courses with
rude instruments. Traveling in a plane at a hundred miles an
hour there is little time for debate. Navigation must be quick
and accurate. Columbus had the whole continent of the western world facing him. The three NC planes were aimed at a
speck in the wide Atlantic; four degrees error and they might
never see the islands.

Behind them, the setting sun streamed across the land, blurring
the outlines of the receding hills, and sweeping out over the
sea in a long sheen of clear light. The water was translucent
and green and icebergs stood out crisply white and motionless.
Ahead, the flyers could see already the darkness spreading over
the east. Presently the shore had gone and in the gathering dusk
it was difficult to see one plane from another. Darkness came
steadily. Riding lights are turned on. In the glow of the small
bulbs of the instrument boards the faces of the pilots look strange
and foreign, under goggles and helmets. Messages are received
and sent. The momentary excitement of the take-off has gone
and in the comforting routine of duties the flight does not seem
so venturesome. Through the thick darkness, for the moon has
not yet risen, the short exhaust pipes glow red hot and the quick
flames at the open ports shine like imprisoned fireflies. The
motors roar monotonously and no sound is sweeter to the men

PROUDLY THE ARGOSY OF THE NC'S HEADED OVER THE ATLANTIC

in the hull suspended below. There is no consciousness of motion, only the wind rushing back and wailing between the struts.

According to reckoning they should be nearing the first of the line of destroyers. The navigator searches with night-glasses the blackness. Suddenly a bright star seems to be falling upward. Then it bursts in a lovely shower of brilliant white light and they know it to be a star-shell fired from the unseen vessel. The pilot leans close to his companion and shouts.

" Pretty nice fireworks, eh? "

The other man nods.

Very satisfactory fireworks. The rocket tells them that their calculated course is correct and all instruments functioning without error. Radio communication is established with the destroyer. Now the moon rises, serene and glowing on the sea-rim. The dark waste of water is lit with the pale fire from the dead world and in the sky the stars lose their brilliance. The horizon line enables the pilots to hold their planes steady and everyone relaxes. Flying by instruments alone is a continual strain; attention must be fixed upon the wavering needle of the altimeter to know if the plane is rising or falling, on the bank and turn indicator to maintain the plane on a horizontal level, but the horizon tells the pilot both of these conditions. He holds the nose of the hull a few inches above it and keeps the long wings parallel. Another star-shell! This time they can see the masthead lights on the ship and the beam of the search-light seeks, but doesn't find them. There are only the roaring motors to guide the crew operating the light, and sound in the dark is deceptive. Regularly they pass the stationed vessels. At no time has any one of the three planes sighted either of the others. But the destroyer radios to the NC-4 that the NC-3 has passed ten minutes before and that the NC-1 has just spoken to the destroyer behind. The commanders begin to believe that all three planes will reach the Azores without accident. . . .

Slowly the moon sank and in that hour before the first light of dawn, weariness came upon the men. Now, they longed for daylight. Hot coffee was poured from the thermos bottles. The men drank it and felt cheered. They ate sandwiches. Imperceptibly the sky brightened.

The pilot of the NC-4 grasped his companion and pointed off the port quarter, where, barely discernible they saw one of the other planes. A short time after, the third one of the fleet was discovered, astern and to the south. By the time the day had come the three ships were in sight of one another; the NC-4 leading the others, and all flying at about a thousand foot level. It appeared as though Commander Towers' dream of leading his flight in formation down to the harbor might come true. The islands ought not to be more than three or four hours away.

But it was not to be!

The crew of the NC-4 glancing back at their sister ships were astonished to see their outlines fade and disappear. It was like magic. One moment they saw them, the sun glinting on the propeller blades, the long dark hulls, the wings shining; then wings and hulls and spinning props were blotted from view. At the same instant their faces became wet and cold. Fog! Hated by all sailors; but to the flyer the one enemy he most fears.

Sea and sky vanished. The fog closed in. There was nothing; no sea, no distance, no direction, no world beneath, only the white pall which made eyesight worse than useless. The pilots stared at the wavering needles on the instrument board. Altimeter rising? Shove her nose down gently. Compass swinging off to the north? Left rudder, and bank a little,—watching the bank and turn dial—level her up. Altimeter falling? Back, easily, on the wheel. Steady, 1450 feet. Over and over, no rest, no momentary relaxing. Vigilance the price of safety. The NC-4 was fortunate in keeping constant radio communication with the destroyers. The NC-1 plunged into storm and fog and could not receive messages because of interference. In a short time they were hopelessly lost. They could not rise above the fog or get below. Rapidly their gasoline supply was consumed as they battled with wind and rain. At last Commander Bellinger decided to make a landing. At the last moment they discovered a sea running fifteen feet high. The NC-1 crashed, straining and tearing the wing-structure. There was no chance of getting back into the air. Helpless they tossed about until the fog rose and they were discovered and rescued by one of the destroyers. The NC-3 was also forced down, but received less damage. The motors would still run and although the sea pounded and tore at the wings they hoped to be able to make Horta safely.

With the motors working they continued to crab slowly across the heavy sea. The storm increased rather than diminished. The radio was disabled for sending, and the situation began to look desperate. Fortunately the wind was blowing toward the islands. The rain came in gusts out of the driving storm, and the hull, racked and twisted by the pressure of wind and waves began to leak. All day and night the hazardous voyage continued. Morning brought no sign of a break in the weather. One of the lower wing tips was torn away and the ship began to list badly.

" Somebody will have to go out on the wing and balance us," said the Commander.

Every man volunteered. The position was so perilous that it was necessary to have the man lashed to the struts. There he lay, while the bitter cold waves broke over him, chilling and bruising. Toward midday they raised Mount Pico, the highest peak of the Azores. But the sea was too heavy for any chance of bucking it over the fifty miles that lay between them and the island of Fayal.

" We've got to try for Ponta Delgada," said the Commander.

The men were worn and exhausted from exposure and the constant struggle to keep the NC-3 afloat. They drank the stale water from the radiators of the wing motors that were no longer running, ate the sodden sandwiches and prepared for another night at sea. The crests of the waves were sometimes twenty feet above the plane and hid the horizon from view. The cold rain numbed their bodies. Luckily the wind held astern and helped them toward the island. Morning came after a night ages long.

" We ought to lift Ponta Delgada soon," said the Commander.

His prediction turned quickly to truth. Ahead they saw the welcome shore line, vineyards, fields and small white stone houses shining on the steep land. When they were sighted a tumult arose on shore and ship. A U. S. Destroyer put out at once, but the crew of the NC-3 refused aid. After fifty-two hours of battling with the Atlantic they crossed the breakwater and taxied into shelter.

They were met by Commander Read and the crew of the NC-4 —the only one of the three planes to make the flight without accident.

Of the little argosy of the air that had flown so bravely from Trepassey Bay only the NC-4 was in condition to continue the flight. The NC-1 had foundered after her crew had been rescued; the NC-3 was battered beyond hope of repairs.

On May 20th the NC-4 rose from the water and began the eight hundred mile trip to Lisbon. Another line of destroyers lay along her course. The trip was without incident. Steadily the great plane forged through the clear air. Commander and crew were elated, but they took no chances. Success seemed assured. The four motors thundered and fishermen on the sea below gazed aloft in astonishment at the dark hull and gleaming wings of the airplane. Slowly at the edge of the blue sea, the shores of the continent of Europe took form. Dusty brown mountains, a harbor filled with shipping. The clean white fronts of houses. Down came the NC-4 in a long steady glide. The heavy hull sent up a shower of spray, bounced once or twice and came to rest. From Lisbon, on schedule time, the NC-4 headed for Plymouth. Two stops were made for minor adjustments and the shore of England lifted from the blue Channel water early on the morning of May 31st.

The ocean had been crossed by an airplane for the first time. Honors were heaped upon Commander Read and his crew, and the first gallant exploit written into the record of the U. S. Navy Aviation Corps.

TWO MEN COME DOWN IN IRELAND

CAPTAIN JOHN ALCOCK AND LIEUTENANT ARTHUR W. BROWN

From St. John's, Newfoundland, to Clifden, Ireland . . . Distance 1960 miles . . . Flying time 16 hours, 12 minutes . . . June 14–15, 1919.

THEY were flying upside down!

Both pilot and navigator realized it at the same moment. Upside down in a fog so thick they could barely see the nacelles of the two motors hung between the long wings of the Vickers-Vimy bomber; upside down over a surging, bitter sea some hundred miles from Ireland and the end of their desperate venture. Or was this the end? Was the huge biplane going into a spin that would whirl them dizzy and sick through the blinding fog to a fatal crash among the wind-torn waves of the North Atlantic? Blood congested their heads. Their two black cats, mascots on the voyage, clawed at the sides of the cockpit in a frantic attempt to keep from being hurled into empty gray space below. Neither man had time to think; Alcock, the pilot, opened wide the motors and shoved the wheel forward. The nose of the bomber dropped and completed the loop by coming back on a level keel. Motors howling, every wire and strut screaming with the strain, the plane hurtled down in a wild plunge through the opaque mist toward the sea. At 300 feet the fog thinned. Alcock caught a flash of white foam and struggled to bring the ship out of its dive. But the terrific momentum carried them along their steep course, lower and lower. The pilot held the wheel back against his chest. Would the elevators never act? Two hundred feet, one hundred! The waves curled up at them, the frayed crests leaped high, driven by the strong southwest wind. " Up! " whispered Alcock. " Come up, old lady! " Just as the spray nipped the

wheels of the under-carriage the plane came under control, and
the disaster was averted.

As if this was the final effort of the Fates to prevent success;
as though, like the heroes of a fairy-tale, these two aviators had
performed all the tasks, accomplished all the deeds of daring,
and triumphed, the plane burst from the fog into the sunlight of
early morning and they saw far ahead a tiny speck of land.
Lieutenant Brown shouted into the communicating phone:
" Eastal Island, or I'm a kee wee! "

But one more danger, unknown to them, awaited at the very
end of the flight.

Now they could see the coast of Ireland rising like a jewel
from the blue sea.   No sight could have been more comforting
than the green grass, low blue misty hills, the tiny white stone
houses and the attenuated wireless masts at Clifden station.
For sixteen hours the two flyers had faced death; four hours they
had flown through fog that extended from sea-level to far beyond
the climbing-range of their machine.   Those hours might well
have shaken the nerves of the bravest flyers.   They had no view
of sea, stars or moon and could not tell whether they were flying
horizontal, climbing, diving or side-slipping into a treacherous
spin that would end abruptly in death.   The instruments they
used were not perfected to the point of the modern bank and
turn and altitude dials of to-day.   It was almost entirely a question of instinct, luck and cool judgment.

There had been rain and sleet until the huge wings were
coated from end to end; the fabric crackled; the fuselage creaked
and groaned under the additional weight, but the two motors

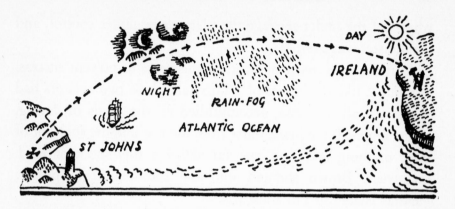

roared steadily.   Navigator Brown checked the course.   Alcock nursed the engines, pitted his skill against the forces of nature and took advantage of a tail-wind that added thirty miles an hour to their normal cruising speed.

The flight had been marked from the start by intrepidity, resourcefulness, courage, good-sportsmanship and independence.

Relaxing, now, with Ireland coming closer and closer, they thought back over the frantic month; from the day, late in May, when the Vickers-Vimy arrived at St. Johns, through all the trials, disappointments and obstacles, to this moment of victory.

The lack of a flying-field had been the first problem and they solved it by building and leveling their own field.   Then the rivalry with the four-motored Hadley-Page that was bound on the same flight, seeking the £10,000 prize offered by the *Daily Mail*.   The Vickers had been assembled before the other plane was ready, but cross-winds blew day after day and to take off in a heavily laden ship from a field barely a quarter mile long under such conditions was inviting a crack-up.   But they did.   Late on

the afternoon of June 14th Alcock persuaded their manager to
let him try.   Minute by minute the motors were put through the
final testing.   The two men crawled into the small cockpit.
Motionless they sat, listening to the deep thunder of the motors.
Full and powerful their exhausts beat upon them, without a miss
or murmur.

" All set? " said Alcock.

Brown nodded.

He ticked off their equipment; ale, sandwiches, hot coffee and
chocolate in thermos bottles; wireless in order, extra flash-light;
the cats.   He leaned down and scratched the back of Twinkle-
toes, glanced at the two yarn dolls hung on each side of the cockpit, Olivette and Ran-Tan-Tan.   In the pocket of his flying coat
was a tiny silver Kewpie.   Symbols of good luck.   The crowds
shrank out of the gale created by the propellers.   Alcock looked
down the short, none too smooth field.   No use waiting; no use
waiting any longer!   A gusty wind blew across the runaway.
The worst possible condition; treacherous, at the moment the
plane lifted, when it had not gotten full flying-speed.   He tested
elevators and ailerons.   " Come on, old lady, let's carry on! "
He waved his hand.

The mechanics jerked the chocks from under the wheels, and
the heavy bomber lurched, yawed, and like a fat woman
waddled slowly across the bumpy turf.   Gradually the speed increased, but the field shrank in an alarming fashion.   Two-thirds
of the distance was behind them and still the machine was rock-
ing over the ground.   Then Alcock felt the plane getting light.
In another moment!   " Come along, old lady!   Come up!

THE FIELD WAS AN IRISH BOG AND THE PLANE WENT OVER ON ITS NOSE

Come up! " The plane felt very light, now. Alcock gently pulled the control-wheel toward him. Space under the wheels! Enough? The trees and fences were shooting up at him. A hundred feet! Barely enough! He lifted the ship clear of a slight rise and saw with relief a long sloping valley. This enabled him to drop the nose a little and get more speed. At the end of the valley he pulled up another hundred feet. Swinging out over the Bay he had room to make an easy turn. A little more altitude and they were safe. The great bomber roared back over the hangar. The crew could see the people waving and shouting. Out over the ocean they headed, on a straight course for Galway Bay, Ireland.

Through fog and rain and storm they went. The wireless was wrecked and this cut them off from the world. East and a little north, they followed the curve of the earth. " Come along, old lady! Carry on! " A British pilot and an American navigator; two black cats, two yarn dolls and a silver Kewpie. Fame and fifty thousand dollars on the far side of the world. . . .

" That's the prettiest sight *I* ever saw," shouted Brown, pointing to Ireland almost below them.

" Right-o! " said the pilot.

Their faces wore broad smiles. Alcock discovered a flat green field and swung in for a landing. Success! All over!

One danger lay ahead of them!

Too late Alcock saw the field he had selected was a swamp. He set the plane down as lightly as he could, but the wheels sank to the hubs, the nose plunged into the soft mire and the long fuselage threshed in an arc above. But their luck still held.

Both were dazed but not hurt. They hung from their safety belts until released by the first arrivals from the wireless station.

England stopped all its activities to heap honors upon the two aviators. Their journey to London was a procession of wild triumph; a succession of demonstrations worthy of their courage and daring.

The Atlantic had been spanned by airplane in the first non-stop flight and the world acclaimed its conquerors.

FROM OCEAN TO OCEAN

LIEUTENANTS JOHN A. MACREADY AND OAKLEY G. KELLY
IN THE "T-2"

*From Long Island, N. Y., to San Diego, California . . .
Distance 2520 miles . . . Flying time 26 hours 50 minutes
. . . May 2–3, 1923.*

THE history of man is bound up in the conquest of space and time. The caravels of Columbus took seventy-one days to cross the Atlantic; the Black Ball packets reduced this to three weeks; the *Great Western* steamship completed the voyage in twelve days; and the *Mauretania* and *Leviathan* sped from Sandy Hook to Plymouth in four days and a few hours.

On land, the United States witnessed similar developments. In 1852, Erza Meeker in his ox-drawn prairie-schooner traveled from coast to coast in five months; the railroads gradually shortened their schedule until the present transcontinental expresses leave New York and arrive at Los Angeles three days and a half later.

Each invention cut the time and eased the journey, but the airplane at one leap outsped all former modes of travel. Alcock and Brown flew the 1900 miles between Newfoundland and Ireland in 16 hours and 12 minutes. Lieutenants Macready and Oakley of the U. S. Air Service hopped from Long Island to San Diego—2500 miles—in 26 hours and 50 minutes. Four years after, this achievement was surpassed with ease.

Both men were from the brood of young pilots developed by the war. They were crack flyers; Lieutenant Macready held the world's altitude record, having forced his plane to its absolute ceiling six and one-half miles above the earth.

It was Lieutenant Kelly who conceived the coast-to-coast

flight.   In the four years that had elapsed since the NC-4 flew to England, planes and motors were being steadily improved.   The flight was of interest to the War Department and when Kelly approached the Army Air Service commanders with his idea, they approved at once.   Kelly wanted Macready as his co-pilot and this suggestion met with instant agreement.   The two flyers began looking about for a suitable plane.

When the war ended Anthony Fokker, Dutch designer of airplanes and one of the recognized leaders in aviation, came to America.   During the early years of the great struggle, Fokker had offered his experience and ability to the English Government.   They declined his aid and he began to build fighting planes for the Germans.   His fast, capable Fokkers were the reason for the German control of the air.   He was always one step ahead of the French and British planes and the Fokker-Triplane was flown by such German aces as the renowned Baron von Richthofen and the best pilots of his Circus.   Fokker had already built several machines for the U. S. Army, and Kelly and Macready selected a Transport T-2.   It was a monoplane, with a great square-ended wing and a long box-shaped fuselage. A 420 H. P. Liberty motor drove the single propeller and the pilots sat in separate cockpits, one behind the other.   They estimated that it was possible to lift the huge ship off the ground with a load of 737 gallons of gas carried in wing and fuselage tanks.

The Weather Bureau said the flight should start from California to secure the help of the prevailing west-east winds.   Kelly and Macready were dubious.

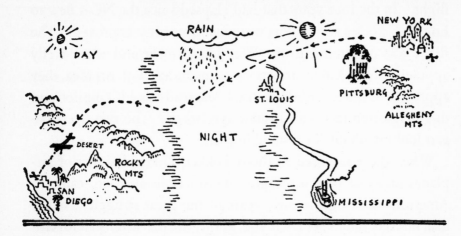

From San Diego they could see the dim high ranges of mountains blocking the sky.

"A couple of thousand feet to clear at Temecula Path right off the bat," said Kelly. "Gas tanks chuck full. . . . We can't lift her, Mac."

"Let's give it a try," said Macready.

They went ahead with their plans. A series of maps with every possible landmark in each state to be crossed was prepared. They were fastened on small boards directly under the eyes of the pilots. The motor was tuned and they were ready.

Until this time, the duration record for planes was 26 hours. Aviation officials thought there was only about one chance in ten for the T-2 to succeed.

Just after dawn on the 4th of October, 1922, the two flyers settled themselves and waved a last good-bye. Kelly was to take the heavy ship off. The throttle was shoved open and the heavy plane lumbered forward. Down the long runway it rolled, gaining speed so slowly that both doubted if it would ever rise.

" Why don't she get light," thought Kelly furiously.   " Come on, baby.   Get light."   Every good pilot can tell when the lift begins to function on the curved upper surface of the wings, before the wheels leave the ground.   The T-2 clung to the earth, bouncing sluggishly.   The motor was wide open.   Its howling exhaust beat back upon their ear-drums, but the cargo of gasoline held the ship to the ground.

" Come on, come on," said Kelly.   He eased the stick and felt a slight response.   The still-spinning wheels of the T-2 showed a streak of light between them and the runway.   Foot by foot they climbed.   A turn was necessary, with only a scant 100 feet of altitude.   Kelly set his jaw.   More pilots are killed by attempting turns close to the ground, than in any other maneuver. He had to hold speed, and that meant diving slightly on the turn.

Gently he banked, ailerons exactly right to prevent slipping or skidding.   At once he sensed the drag of the lowered wing. Down went the nose.   The land leaped up at him, as he leveled the plane.   He held the ship down until they were barely twenty feet in the air.   They were around!   Now he had a chance to recover some height.   He forced the plane gradually up and swung east of the mountains.   They got through Temecula Pass safely, but the fog began gathering.   Thicker and thicker it descended, hiding the winding valley, dangerous in the clearest weather.

Kelly passed a note back to Macready.

THE MOUNTAINS WERE RISING FASTER THAN THE PLANE COULD CLIMB

" Call it off? "

His companion agreed.

Disconsolately they headed toward San Diego.

They hated to go back. It was an anti-climax. They felt foolish. Macready glared at the foothills as they slid the T-2 down to lower altitude. " I'd rather play around here for a day or two," he thought. But that idea held a certain monotony. He wanted an objective. " We might stay up long enough to break the duration record." That was a real plan. He scribbled a note to Kelly and back came the answer. " O. K. Let's go to it."

They flew for thirty-five hours breaking the previous record by eight hours, but because of a technicality, their record was not accepted and the two pilots continued to plan for another attempt at a transcontinental flight.

A month later they took off for the second trial. They were more fortunate. They followed the winding passages and crossed the lower mountains without any trouble. In Arizona their first serious difficulties began. The ground rose faster than the plane could climb. Cross-winds made the air bumpy and uncertain. There were times when 50 feet of altitude was the limit of the heavy plane. They could not relax for a moment. The bottom would drop out, and the T-2 would hurtle toward volcanic rocks, black and dead and jagged. Dusk found them, barely able to cross the highest ridge of mountains. Night brought clouds, threatening weather and a nervous sense of isolation. They kept their course by instinct and good fortune. There was a tornado raging in Kansas, a wall of wind sweeping

down houses and trees. The edge whirled down upon the labor-
ing T-2. Rain and lightning added to their terrors. The flashes
blinded them. The thunder drowned the roar of the Liberty
motor. Rain steamed across the wind-shields, blurred their
scanty vision. Communication was impossible. When Kelly
was worn out he shook the controls and Macready took over the
task. They did not dare attempt a landing. Salvation lay in
keeping the plane afloat until morning, and they succeeded.
Kelly was jubilant. He had a vision of eating dinner in New
York that evening, but with the light, Macready in the forward
cockpit just behind the motor, saw, suddenly, the end of their
gallant effort. The water-jackets on two cylinders were cracked,
and that essential fluid spurting from the hot motor.

They landed at Indianapolis.

" Twice," said Kelly gloomily.

" The third time wins," said Macready.

He was correct.

The two flyers spent the winter at Dayton, where they finally
broke the duration record. Spring revived their determination
to make a non-stop coast-to-coast hop.

"No matter what the Weather Man says," Macready said,
" this time we go east-west. No plane can stand the strain of
crawling over those passes with everything full up. If we start
from New York we'll be dry and light by the time we hit the
high spots. What do you say? "

" I've figured it just that way," said Kelly.

They tuned up their plane and took off from Roosevelt Field.
The start presented its inevitable danger. The first trial failed.

The T-2 would not rise.   The second time they got off, but the first three hours was a desperate battle to keep the plane in the air.   At nightfall, they encountered a little rain, but presently, the clouds broke and the moon shone cheerfully upon them.   By morning the T-2 was well into New Mexico.

The ground below began to rise; ahead foothills lifted into mountains.   But their plan had been correct.   Each hour the T-2 lightened its load.   It was as though they were climbing an invisible highway that mounted parallel with the solid roads upon the world below.   Up went the T-2; and the altitudes marked on the pilot's maps followed the plane.   They swung into the mountains seeking a pass that would lead them into Arizona.   At least it was discovered.   Across the desert they flew and into the rich green Imperial Valley.   One range of mountains remained to be conquered.   The T-2, tanks almost empty, took it like a bird.

"Up and over," said Kelly joyously.   "Come on; jump, baby."

From their 8000 feet elevation they could see San Diego and the end of their flight.

"Let her ride," thought Macready, and shoved the nose down. The T-2 howled toward victory.   Down the long, invisible slide of the air, the plane shot.   The wind screamed by and almost drowned the roar of the motor.   The ground seemed to leap upward in great bounds.   From confused patches of color, it became fields, orange-groves, roads, gardens and houses.   Behind them, the conquered mountains lifted higher and higher.   Over the city they roar; above the buildings where every window was filled with cheering people, and all the traffic halted by crowds gathered in the streets. Bank and dip in salute! Straighten out for Rockwell Field, a long rushing glide, motor throttled, wheels and skids, kicking up dust-twirls in a perfect landing. Twenty-six hours and 50 minutes from New York to California.

NINE DAYS IN A SEAPLANE

Lt. Commander John Rodgers and Crew of the "PN9-1"

From San Francisco, California, to Kauai Island, Hawaii . . .
Actual flight 1850 miles . . . Sailed on ocean approximately
450 miles . . . August 31–Sept. 8, 1924.

"LANDING! Landing! Landing! Landing!"
The radio flung the terse message continuously into space until the antenna struck the surface of the water. The great seaplane was coming down fast and the five men of the crew braced themselves for the shock, but the pilot stalled neatly at the last moment and set the heavy boat-shaped hull lightly as a feather upon the crest of a long Pacific roller. To bring a flying-boat safely to rest among waves running ten feet high is a delicate maneuver at all times; when done on a "dead stick" with no spinning propellers to create a stream of air that gives speed and control, it becomes an art.

Lieutenant Byron J. Connell, the pilot of the U. S. Navy seaplane PN9-1, shoved back his goggles and glared morosely at the cool, gray water of the Pacific lapping within a foot or two of where he sat instead of being eight hundred feet below. For twenty hours he had shared the responsibility of flying the craft with his co-pilot, Pope. He was tired, fatigued with the roar and vibration of the two motors howling on either side of the control-cockpit; and his weariness was increased by the sudden termination of their effort to fly from San Francisco to Hawaii after covering almost nineteen hundred miles without an accident.

"Where do we go from here?" he said.

None of his companions answered. Commander Rodgers, radioman Stantz, Bowlin, in charge of the engines, and the other pilot, Pope; they were equally depressed and exhausted. They sat, limply, staring at the empty ring of the horizon. The regular swell lifted the silent plane, the slight wind swung it lazily into the trough of the sea, the next wave rolled under— the slow cradle of the vast ocean rocked this curious man-made bird, helplessly adrift, gasoline tanks bone dry, and no power to operate the radio that would send its tapping message to the destroyers watching anxiously for passage of the plane. Here was the humiliating end to months of labor and training. And added to their sorrows was the knowledge that only two hundred and fifty miles remained to be covered; barely three hours of flying. If they had been able to pick up the trade wind that blew approximately from east to west, at this time of the year there would have been sufficient fuel to make the islands.

" How about setting the balloon jib? " said Connell.

Commander Rodgers grinned; Pope lifted his head and chuckled. They all felt better and began discussing plans for some sort of action. Their disappointment was ignored, and there was no reason, as yet, for apprehension. Behind them were all the traditions of the United States Navy; and these were naval men, trained, disciplined, resourceful, courageous, hardened to physical dangers, accustomed to difficult situations, and inculcated with the idea of duty which meant obedience and the submerging of the individual for the common good, without the loss of personal initiative or daring. Any one of the five would have sacrificed his life for the others; now each one brought his particular knowledge and talents to the effort of reaching land or discovering one of the attending destroyers. Commander Rodgers made rapid calculations.

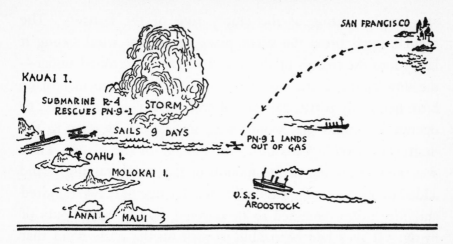

"We're in latitude 24° 20', longitude 157° 58'," he said. "The *Aroostook* ought to be within sixty miles. Kauai is the nearest island. We'll rig sails and head for it but we'll probably be picked up in an hour or two."

"I hope we are," Pope said. "I want to fly in, not come crawling along like some canal boat."

"Oh, we'll fly in all right. We can refuel from the *Aroostook.*"

"Crawling is all right by me," said Bowlin, "if we have to crawl."

They rigged canvas in rude sails between the wings and the heavy plane swung slowly off before the wind and started to sail the two hundred and fifty miles to Kauai. A little ripple sprang out from the blunt nose of the duralumin hull and trailed encouragingly astern. They all felt quite cheerful and realized they were hungry. Stantz and Bowlin got out the kite which carried a radio-antenna and managed to set it sailing above the ship but no messages came over and Stantz, worn out, curled up and went to sleep. When he awoke it was almost sundown. He sat up and rubbed his eyes.

" Where's the kite? " he said.

" Kite? " said Bowlin. " What kite? "

" What kite? " Stantz glared suspiciously. " The kite for the radio."

" Oh, *that* kite," grinned Bowlin cheerfully. " I saw it go into a nose-dive about an hour ago. A peach of a nose-dive, Stantz, my lad. Crash into the jolly old Pacific. The last I saw, a shark was wearing it for a sun-bonnet."

" You didn't try to save it? " said Stantz.

" Oh, sure. I yelled at it. I waved my arms. I shouted— ' Pull up on the stick! Pull up.' But it was in a flat spin by that time. You know what a flat spin in a kite is, Stantz ——"

" Oh, dry up," said the radioman.

" I am," said Bowlin mournfully. " I'm so dry my mouth is full of cotton."

" I ought to have stayed awake," Stantz said remorsefully. " I knew something would happen."

" That's all right," said Commander Rodgers. " No one could have done anything. A heavy gust snapped the line and away it went."

The wind dropped at sunset, as it does usually, and then freshened again. They turned on the riding lights of the upper wing and divided the night into five watches. The Commander took the first watch and the others arranged themselves as comfortably as possible in the cramped space. At daybreak they were all awake scanning the gray waste for a trail of smoke or the sight of the top masts of a sailing vessel.

" Not a thing," said Connell, " not even a gull."

" Well, boys," said Rodgers, " how about breakfast? Appetites hearty? "

They grinned. The sandwiches were too mouldy to eat, except for pieces of the crust. They sat in the flat space above the lower wing and munched the bits of stale bread and drank sparingly of the water supply.

" Coffee's not up to scratch," said Bowlin. " I'll have to speak to that cook again."

" Fire her," said Pope. " Tell her to pack up and leave at once."

" By train? " said Connell.

" Oh, no, by airplane! It's the fastest form of modern transportation."

" Well, I feel better," said Stantz. " I'm going to find some way of rigging up a receiving wire or you can ask for my resignation."

" You can't get enough length, can you? " said Bowlin. " And how about grounding? "

" I've figured a way, I think," Stantz said. " There's some waxed cord aboard. We can string the wire from the bow to the wing tips and back to the aft cockpit."

" Heave that end of wire," said Connell.

He took the copper wire and crawled out on one wing while Bowlin crawled on the other to balance the plane. Connections were made and the waxed cord replaced the missing insulators.

Stantz clamped on the head phones, and bent over his makeshift aerial.

" Here they come," he said.

He wrote rapidly and passed the slips of paper for the others to read. The messages were calls to the PN9-1, and instructions for the destroyers to start a systematic search.

" They're coming over pretty loud," said Stantz. " They can't be so far away." But when positions were given he realized the distance was greater than he thought.

" That won't do us much good," said the Commander. " They're too far south. Maybe they'll shift up a bit if they find no signs."

This contact with the world was at once heartening and discouraging. To know that every effort was being made cheered them, but to realize that the search was misdirected and that they were powerless to help, depressed them again. The morning passed slowly. They were quieter now and the bantering died away. Water was carefully rationed. At intervals one of the men dozed but either Stantz or Bowlin was constantly in the rear cockpit listening to radio messages. In the afternoon the wind freshened and a choppy sea began tearing the fabric on the lower wing tips.

" We'd better cut it away," said Connell.

Commander Rodgers considered.

" No more than necessary," he said. He still hoped they would meet one of the destroyers, refuel and fly into Hawaii. It was a ticklish job, working far out on the wings of the unsteady craft, but they accomplished it safely.

The weather looked unsettled. The sun went down in a hazy west and they watched the sky, feeling uneasy. Stantz called from the radio instrument and passed a message forward. It read:

" PN9-1. Thought we saw your flare ahead. If you pick this up, please fire star-shell or show light."

The radio had been sent from the *Aroostook.*

" Fire off a shell, Connell," said the Commander.

The Lieutenant took the Véry pistol from its holster and went out on the nose of the hull. They watched, tense with excitement. The little glowing ball shot wavering into the upper darkness, burst in a shower of white light. Each man took a section of the horizon and inspected it for an answering signal. The minutes dragged by, night came; two or three hours passed but no light shone in response. Discouraged they arranged the customary watches and sank into an exhausted sleep.

At dawn they were awakened by a wild shout from Bowlin on lookout.

" Smoke! There's a ship dead ahead! "

Instantly every man was alert, eagerly anticipating their rescue. Visible above the horizon line were the top masts of a steamer and a thin plume of smoke trailing.

" See if you can pick up anything from her," ordered the Commander.

Stantz leaped for the radio and snapped on the earphones. They watched his anxious face, wrinkled as he strained to hear the code message which might give them information of the vessel's intentions. No word came. It was discouraging. Slowly the steamer forged ahead, never altering its course, the hull remaining always out of sight, and the spars moving along as though the ship were sailing under water. Desperately Stantz tried various methods of tapping out a signal but to no effect. The masts began to vanish. Slowly they dropped below the horizon.

"Just as though she were sinking," said Connell gloomily.

After the steamer had gone the crew of the PN9-1 were convinced that their strange voyage might last a great deal longer than they had believed. They held a council of war and decided to give up the idea of flying to Hawaii, even should they be picked up.

"We might as well face it," said the Commander. He looked at the four men squatting about on the rolling hull. Their faces were burned to a bright raw pink by the three days of exposure to sun and wind of the open Pacific. Bloodshot eyes, chins covered with whiskers, hair unkempt and matted with salt-damp, told the story of hardship. They were haggard, hungry, and feeling the first pangs of that worst of all tortures, thirst. But there was no sign of fear; no weakness of spirit. They were quiet, but that very silence was filled with determination. "This is a good gang," thought their Commander proudly. "If anyone can come through, they will." Stantz, who had been ill ever since the landing, had made no word of complaint, neither had he failed to take his full share of duties. He said:

With tanks empty the PN9-1 glided toward the Sea

"There's just a chance, maybe, of generating enough power to get out an S. O. S."

"I've thought of that, too," said Lieutenant Connell. "It's a slim chance, though."

"We'll try it," said the Commander. "But first we've got to look at this squarely. There's a good two hundred miles of sailing ahead of us. Say four days. There isn't enough mouldy bread left to feed a fly. By to-morrow we'll be down to the last drop of water, unless we hit a shower. Probably we will. Perhaps we won't. The fleet is moving gradually away from us. They've figured our drift all wrong, I guess. It will be dumb luck if they hit on us. This weather doesn't please me a bit. We may be in for a big blow. And if —— Well, let's not count chickens yet. That's how it stands."

"We've got to rip off the rest of the fabric on these lower wings," Pope said. "Or else this sea is going to shake every rib loose."

"That's first," said Rodgers. "Then we'll try the radio, and see if we can hook a fish or two."

"A fish," said Bowlin dreamily. "A beautiful fish broiled and garnished ——"

"Shut up," said Stantz, "or we'll use you for bait."

"Me for bait?" Bowlin answered. "Stantz, my lad, no self-respecting fish would even sniff at me, much less nibble."

"Let's get the fabric off," said Rodgers, laughing. "And then we'll toss a coin whether Stantz or Bowlin should be used for bait."

It wasn't an easy task, lying out on the wings, stripping

away the tough, tightly-stretched covering.   A brisk sea tumbled about the plane, and the crests broke down sharply over the men. When it was accomplished the PN9-1 rode easier.   Then Connell and Stantz began planning a way to generate current for the radio, and the others attempted to lure stray fish to their destruction with bits of the rotten salt-beef on bent pins.

The hot September day dragged into evening without any success on the part of the fishermen.   Connell and Stantz were trying to take one of the flywheel starters off the motor, with the intention of fastening it to the shaft of the radio generator.

" If it holds," said Connell, " we might be able to crank it up to a speed that would let Stantz get off at least an S. O. S. and position."

It was a long hard job to remove the flywheel and their tools were not the best for the work.   Darkness came and they had not succeeded in detaching the wheel.

The night passed into the morning of the fourth day.   Sharks appeared and followed the disabled plane.

" Aren't they pretty? " said Bowlin.   " Look at that nice little fellow.   Eighteen feet, if he's an inch."

Late in the afternoon they rigged the detached flywheel to the generator shaft for the experiment.   If it worked they would have rescue planes about them in an hour or two.   It failed! The wheel tore loose and there was an end of their last possible hope of rescue.   They accepted the failure with grim good-humor.

The weather continued to thicken, but the crew of the PN9-1 were seamen as well as flyers.   They took in sail and threw out a sea-anchor, holding the nose of the plane safely into the wind. No one could sleep, though, and the plane tossed badly, wracking the wing-structure. Suddenly the Commander shouted:

" Rain! It's raining! "

They spread a piece of canvas to catch the falling drops but the rain-clouds blew by and scarcely wet the surface. The water situation was desperate. All the men were weak from thirst, hunger and exposure. They moved wearily to change the sails. The sea was so rough that it was necessary to have someone constantly at the control-wheel. Life-lines were strung to prevent anyone falling overboard. Two days passed and the last drop of water was gone. The next night they saw the search-lights on Oahu Island. Calculations showed it to be a hundred miles away. Still, something had to be done.

The PN9-1 had been able to sail only before the wind. This meant they would be blown past the island. They rigged a leeboard and found the strange sailing-boat could be turned at a slight angle from the wind, enough to reach the island. With dawn they could see the island although their reckoning showed it to be fifty miles away.

" That's the prettiest sight I ever saw," said Pope.

" But we can't make it," Commander Rodgers said quietly.

" Can't make it? "

" Not a chance. The only thing to do is to head for Kauai."

" But that's over a hundred miles."

" It's our only hope."

They altered the course. Slowly Oahu faded into the blue distance. The sea-rim formed, unbroken, about the tiny speck of plane with its five exhausted men. Silence returned. The sharks followed lazily. The crew did the necessary tasks with only as little effort as possible.

Commander Rodgers stared moodily at the endless lapping water. He was responsible for men and ship. The decisions were his to make. An error on his part might mean disaster. Was he right in selecting Kauai instead of Oahu? Fifty miles more meant another day at sea. His men were reaching the point of complete physical exhaustion. Water! That would give them new strength and spirits. He shook his head impatiently. Things were darkening about him. The sunlight was not as bright. Were his eyes going bad? Lifting his head he saw a great black cloud sweeping over the sun. He gave a shout of joy. This *was* rain. No doubt of it. His voice roused the others. Scarcely had they spread the canvas when the storm broke. The rain slashed down with tropic violence. They filled thermos bottles and canteens and drank the cool sweet rain. It entered the pores of their racked bodies and revived them. They felt cheerful again, optimistic.

" That's an omen," said Connell. " We'll make it sure."

They knew they would. Stantz tried to whistle through lips cracked and blistered by the sun.

" Just think, Stantz, my lad," said Bowlin. " This time to-morrow you'll be getting outside of a six-pound beefsteak."

He was not far wrong.

All night they sailed and by morning were close to Kauai. But a new difficulty arose. The two harbors were on the far side of the island. Before them rose a rocky coast with the heavy sea of the Pacific lashing itself into a white turmoil at the base. No place there to land.

"Somebody ought to spot us, now," said Connell.

They took a bucket and filled it with damp pieces of fabric, lit them and sent up smoke signals. Now began the most nerve-racking time of the whole strange adventure. A few miles away was safety, food, rest. They could see the trees, the rocks, the high flung foam; almost they imagined it possible to distinguish people. But they could not hope to reach the land by their own efforts. The waves would crush the PN9-1 to splinters, and, in their weakened condition, in all probability they would drown. Yet, if no one saw them, they were at the mercy of wind and current, and both were carrying them past the island into the open Pacific. Every man realized their position and they waited in grim silence the result of the rising column of smoke.

Suddenly Bowlin shouted: "Hey! There's a sub."

Directly astern the blunt black steel snout of a submarine lifted out of a welter of broken water. The extraordinary voyage was ended. From the conning tower the officers emerged out of the undersea boat. The PN9-1 was taken in tow and in a short time was safely at anchor. Although the flight had failed, the adventure was a tribute to the designers and builders of the seaplane at the Philadelphia Navy Yard, and the fame of Commander Rodgers and his crew became greater when the long tale of hardship and courage was told.

Eighteen hundred and fifty miles the PN9-1 flew from San Francisco until, fuel exhausted by continuous headwinds, it had descended to the surface of the water. During the nine days between that moment and the appearance of the submarine, the plane had sailed four hundred and fifty miles additional, survived heavy seas that would have proved dangerous to a sailing-vessel of the same size. The strange voyage of the PN9-1 has become an epic of the United States Navy.

LINDBERGH

COLONEL CHARLES A. LINDBERGH IN THE " SPIRIT OF ST. LOUIS "

From Roosevelt Field, L. I., to Le Bourget Field, France . . . Distance 3610 miles . . . Flying time 33 hours, 30 minutes . . . May 20–21, 1927.

A FLEET of fishing-boats heaved sluggishly on the long Atlantic swells. They were clumsy, bluff-bowed boats with thick masts and heavy, patched sails. The day's catch had been a poor one and they were getting under way for the return to Irish harbors from which they had come. Blocks creaked, ropes whined, and the sails slatted in the westerly wind. The late afternoon sun dipped toward the sea line and long shadows of rigging rippled across the oily green water. High over the mastheads a gull squalled. The sailors moved slowly about their work, and the familiar sounds of the sea; timbers complaining, the slogging wash of broad sterns settling into the trough of a wave, were scarcely heard. A hundred miles of water lay between them and their villages; a day's voyaging if the wind did not freshen.

"A bad trip," said the captain of one of the luggers. "It's herself who will be missing a new gown, an' . . ." He stopped abruptly. "In the name of the Saints, what's that?"

The air was roaring and drumming in their ears. A hurricane? The wind blew gently; the sky was cloudless. A man began shouting and wildly waving. Sailors sprang into the rigging and blinked under shielding hands back into the sun-path. Something moved in the brilliance. Gull or monster? Swiftly it sped toward them, like a strange arrow shot from some distant world. The rails of the fishing-boats were hung with gaping faces. The bowl of the sky reverberated with the throbbing metallic explosions.

" An airplane," gasped the captain.

Out of the sun it dove, silver and shining, its single wing glinting, the propeller twin spindles of light. Fifty feet from the water and parallel to the lugger its dive ended. Gracefully the wing tilted until the astounded sailors could see a dark rectangular window in the fuselage, a lean young face peering at them and a long arm waving. They were too stupefied to do more than lift their arms. Twice the plane circled the boat. Underneath the wing was painted NX-211 in huge black letters. The pilot signaled frantically but the sail rs could not understand. Then he waved in a last half-salute. The plane zoomed beautifully, leveled off and headed toward Ireland. They watched it dwindle to a speck and vanish.

" Aye," said the captain, drawing down his long clean-shaven lip, " this is a mad world. Flying bits of machinery over the sea. Where did it come from, do ye think? "

" From across the ocean," called a sailor. There was a great uproar of hooting and laughter. The sailor, Dennis, had a wild mind; always he was imagining something outlandish and foolish. True, years before, just after the war was ended, one of the flying machines had come, winging like a crazy bird from the far country of America and taken a header in a bog near to Clifden. But there were two of the flying chaps in it and they could stand trick and trick at the tiller of the thing, whilst this had but a single young 'un peering from its cabin. No, the man Dennis had a neat fancy, but they couldn't be taken in with such nonsense. From somewhere in Ireland he had flown, or perhaps one of the great English flying-fields such as .   .   .

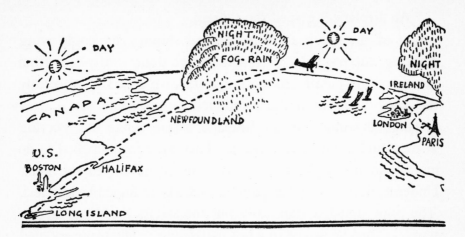

" What name is it, Dennis? "

" Croyden, you mean? "

" Aye, Croyden Field."

Sails were trimmed, courses laid, the little fleet got heavily away on its long sail.

By the time five miles had flowed under the plunging fore-foot, their unexpected visitor was roaring above the incredible green hills of Ireland. Men and women ran from cottages with their white walls of stone, and dark roofs of thatch, waving caps and aprons. Wireless and cable were hurling the news across the world.

" He's over! "

" Lindbergh's made it! "

" Are you sure? "

" Just now. Over the radio."

" Sighted above Ireland, you say? "

" Yes, and flying a bee-line for Paris."

" A hundred miles an hour and better, he's making."

The world-cities, New York, London, Paris, Berlin had seen no such universal excitement since the Armistice. But the thrill was not only for the city dwellers; fishermen on the decks of Gloucester schooners shouted the news; small villages lost among the Jersey pine-woods, heard it over radios; it spread from porch to porch, through towns in the level monotony of the mid-west; it was carried to adobe huts in the Arizona desert, to ranches on the Texas ranges, to Colorado silver mines, shacks along the Yukon, to the desert country, on the Continental Divide, along Death Valley, among the orange groves of California . . . "Lindbergh's over!" Cowboys at Manuelito, tourists on the platform at Albuquerque, the switch-tender at Wickenberg, the half-breed guide at Little Deer, the banker in Wall Street shouted the news: " Lindbergh's made it."

Lindbergh!

Three weeks before none of these people had heard the name of Lindbergh. Now it was written, imperishable upon the record of man. A young fellow, barely twenty-five, had become the most important figure in the world. Here was Romance without parallel.

How little is really known of this tall sinewy youth, at once the most popular and the most enigmatic figure before the public gaze. The facts of his life are not so different from many another. He wanted to fly. Planes droned through his dreams, waking and sleeping. He would fly. He left college and barnstormed with an aviator. Then he bought an old plane, took a few lessons and began. His adventures were not extra-ordinary. Finally he went to the army training school at Kelly Field. Here his genius first was noticed. He completed the course with honors. His was a pure flying sense, backed by superb skill and courage. When he strapped on the safety-belt, he became, literally, part of his ship. The volatile reaches of the air were his natural home. His sense of direction was as true as that of a bird, and as a bird adjusts, without thought, its wings, to the varying pressure of the winds, so this young man controlled his plane. He was never oppressed by the feeling of solitude and loneliness, as are so many flyers; the vast untenanted spaces of the heavens meant freedom. He did not miss the com-panionship of his fellow-creatures, plodding the earth below, although he liked them and was liked in turn; for the wind in the landing-wires and the deep-roaring motor, were friendly and satisfying voices.

To Lindbergh, there was none of the monotony that so many pilots feel when they make flights of any length over familiar distances. When the wheels of his ship parted from the solid earth, he seemed quite willing never to return. As one veteran flyer of the air-mail said: "He would have liked to fly all day and sleep all night on a cloud." Even this was hardly an apt description, for night-flying was to him more fascinating than travel by day. Then he was truly detached from the earth, which seemed to him as foreign as do the skies to those who have spent their lives among the normal habitats of men.

Lindbergh entered the air-mail service after the completion of his army training course. He sat in his plane, watching the mail being stowed in its compartment, listening to the throttled mutter of the engine. Before him the landing field seemed drenched in a brilliant moonlight, a colorless glare spread by the huge arcs. At the far corner the beacon spun its slow beam into the black sky. The mail plane was headed up-wind, ready to start without waste of time. An official came to the plane, and the pilot leaned his helmeted head down to hear. The official had the latest weather report.

"Some local rain near Springfield, Slim," he said. "Visibility about three quarters. Northwest wind on the ground, blowing twelve miles; northeast at 2000 feet, blowing twenty. O. K.?"

The pilot nodded, adjusted his goggles, opened up the motor watching the revolutions-per-minute dial, listening to the steady, clear howl of the exhaust pipes from the nine cylinders. Throttling it again, he waved his hand. Chocks were jerked from before the wheels. The motor roared with power and the slip-stream swept back in a solid current. The tail of the plane came up, and with a leaping swirl the ship was off the ground and gone.

"That boy," said a mechanic, "just kicks 'em off, load or no load."

"He's got the sweetest touch on a stick of anyone I ever saw," said the pilot who had brought the mail over the previous stretch. "It's not human! I've seen him come in with a cross-wind blowing that would almost tear your hair off and set his ship down without a quiver. There's somethin' uncanny about the way that boy does his stuff. If you ask me, I'd say, some-

where he had a great-grandfather or somebody with some con-
cealed wings, maybe!"

"You read too many Tarzan books," said the field manager,
laughingly.

"Well, maybe," said the pilot. "But you've got to admit
Slim is just about as good as they come."

"He's a little better than that," the manager said. "We'll
hear about him some day. Mark my words."

"Sure," said the pilot. "That's what I'm tryin' to tell you.
Only that don't get me something to eat. Say, you know, I get
so howlin' hungry on this run. When it's easy going, like to-
night, I begin to think of what I'd like to eat; a nice steak, say,
with bacon and mushrooms; or a peck of steamed clams with hot
butter, the way we used to have 'em back home in Connecticut,
or maybe something else. And by the time I'm due over Musun
I'm hungry enough to chew my gloves. Some day a wise boy
will set up a few lunch-balloons and make a lot of jack from
fellows with appetites like mine."

Minutes before the riding lights of Lindbergh's mail plane
had vanished. Somewhere in the gloomy vault of the night he
was flying north at 90 miles an hour. The dim flow of the lights
on the instrument board outlined his quiet face. The wind-
shield deflected the blast of air that rushed in a gale along the
rounded flanks of the fuselage. Overhead a few stars shone
feebly, blurred by a high floating mist. Below he saw an occasional pocket of lights marking some small town. The air-
way beacons were passed at regular intervals. The showers re-
ported near Springfield had passed and the night seemed clearer

as he came in for a landing. The plane was refueled, mail
loaded and discharged, and he was ready to continue.

"You may hit some muck, further on!" said the weather man.
"Fog and some rain, but it's expected to clear away near
Chicago."

Lindbergh again nodded. The admiring ground crew
watched his steep, thundering take-off.

This time the weather did not clear. Fog shut in and, instead
of rain, a light snow began falling. Before he reached Peoria
he suspected that a landing there would be impossible. It was.
Only a faint glow marked the town. Lindbergh decided to keep
on to Chicago. Perhaps the storm did not extend that far. He
wasn't very hopeful but there was no choice. Steadily the fog
thickened and the snow-flurries came faster and denser. Know-
ing the fog went right down to the ground, he thought perhaps
he could climb above it. He forced the heavy plane to 14,000
feet and there was no break. Gray-white, impenetrable, the
storm surrounded him. To reach Chicago also became impossible. Only a few gallons of gas remained. Quietly Lindbergh
loosened the safety-belt, snapped the switch and in the sudden
silence, stepped to the cowling of the cockpit and plunged into
the unsubstantial sea of the air. He pulled the rip-cord and over
him the silk parachute opened like a gigantic mushroom. Slowly
he floated through snow and fog toward the unseen earth. He
knew that when he had leaped the altimeter of the plane was
near 12,000 feet, but in the murky descent he lost all sense of
time or distance and struck heavily across a barbed-wire fence.
Fortunately his thick flying suit protected him and he arose

shaken but unhurt and started out on the first duty of an air-mail
pilot, to secure and deliver the mail.

In this exacting and dangerous flying, Lindbergh received the
schooling that was to be of inestimable value to him in his great
achievement. On his job of carrying the mail, he learned to
fly his plane through rain, fog, sleet, wind and darkness, training
himself to do with a minimum of sleep, keeping his physical
condition to the fine point of an athlete preparing for a contest,
gathering knowledge of navigation by instruments alone when
all trace of the earth had vanished and he was " flying blind."

The nickname of " Lucky " has no relation to Lindbergh. It
is one of those catch-phrases exploited by newspapers. " Lucky "
he may have been but his " luck " was the result of days and
months of careful, patient study, of intelligent preparation, of
the most thorough practical training, of dangers faced and conquered. No pilot calls Lindbergh " lucky " except as a casual,
joking term of admiration. Ask any of them if he is " lucky,"
and the answer comes:

" He's a great flyer. There isn't anything he doesn't know
about the game. There are pilots in the Army and Navy who
can stunt better than he can; there are chaps who can fly from
here to Europe; but no one has *all* the qualifications to the degree that Lindbergh has. Didn't he step in, without any practice, and lead the Three Musketeers—the best Army pursuit
pilots—at the Los Angeles show, after the unfortunate accident
to Lieutenant Williams? And a good job he made of it. No,
there are plenty good flyers in this country, but only one

of Lindbergh. Lucky? He doesn't need to be; he makes his own luck."

When Lindbergh had secured backing for his attempt to fly from New York to Paris and win the $25,000 prize offered by M. Raymond Orteig he went to the Ryan Aircraft Company and asked them to design a plane for him. Here he introduced several revolutionary features of construction. All planes are designed to give the pilot maximum visibility. The importance of being able to see when landing is vital to safety. Yet Lindbergh insisted that his plane should have the gas tank placed before him, closing solidly the nose of the ship. On each side of the fuselage beside him was a small window. For seeing ahead he used a periscope. And he flew the plane with the same ease he would have flown an open-cockpit machine. Outside of this radical change, the plane was a conventional Ryan monoplane driven by a Wright Whirlwind 220 H. P. motor. It was painted silver and christened the *Spirit of St. Louis*.

Lindbergh was ready to go.

Beyond the low sandy point of Long Island lay the Atlantic, passively awaiting those who were to dare its path of wind, fog, sleet and rain. Already on the tragic records of death names of bold adventurers who failed were being inscribed. Rene Fonck's great plane had crashed, burst into flame, consuming two men, without ever having lifted from the earth. Lieutenants Davis and Wooster in *The American Legion* took off but the overloaded plane would not gain altitude. Flyers did not understand clearly then that a plane actually too heavy to fly

The "Spirit of St. Louis" circled the plunging fishing boat

may be forced to rise to a height approximating the wing-span, but will not go higher, and inevitably must crash. *The American Legion* demonstrated this curious condition. Lieutenant Davis at the controls found himself forced to attempt a turn. With superb skill he circled his ship, but could not regain speed. A forced landing was made. Still there was a chance, but the plane struck in a swamp, turned over, and its crew died strapped in their seats. Tragedy and misfortune rode with the flyers. Commander Byrd's tri-motored Fokker monoplane crashed in a test flight, injuring Byrd, Noville and Floyd Bennett. Of all the contestants Clarence Chamberlain, pilot of the *Columbia,* remained untouched by disaster. Then from France two of the most noted sons of the Tricolor set out in *The White Bird.* Westward they flew into the sunset and no word of them was ever received. Nungesser and Coli became immortal names.

The hot afternoon of May 12th was broken by a thunderstorm. On Roosevelt Field planes were wheeled quickly into hangars. Pilots, mechanics and spectators ran for shelter. The rain ended quickly. Eastward the wind drove the dark storm clouds. Dazzling the sun streamed from under the black rim, glinting on the rain-swept grass. Out of the sudden glory of the sun came a silver plane, shining and wet. It made the customary circles of the field and glided softly to earth. There it stood, brilliant in the radiance, alone on the wide field; a symbol.

" It's that fellow, Lindbergh! "

Word of his record-breaking flight from San Diego to St. Louis had been telegraphed east. Pilots crowded about his craft; spectators came from all parts of the field. Lindbergh swung out of the small cabin. Chamberlain welcomed him.

" Who's going with you? " he said.

" Nobody," answered Lindbergh.

They stared at him incredulously, while he went quietly about his final preparations. Flying alone. That meant a minimum of thirty hours without sleep; thirty hours of the most nerve-racking attention. Heads were shaken dubiously. It looked like suicide of the wildest sort.

" I'm used to it," Lindbergh said. " Lack of sleep doesn't worry me."

Apparently nothing worried him. Calmly, confidently, he prepared. He was certain and the character of his certainty was impressive.

" He'll make it," pilots told one another.

He even bought a return steamer ticket. The entire nation was captivated by his courage, his modesty. On the evening of the twentieth of May he said:

" I'm going to-morrow morning."

After three hours' sleep, he appeared at the field. The prospect was not encouraging. The fog had lifted, but a drizzle of rain fell and the runway was broken by puddles and heavy with water. The *Spirit of St. Louis* was hauled to the start. Tanks were filled. A dim glow in the east marked the coming of dawn. Byrd and Chamberlain came to wish him farewell. A little group of people huddled under the rain, chilled and shivering, but unwilling to miss the beginning of the greatest epic of the air. A feeling of awe descended upon them. There was an aura of splendor about the flight that lifted it beyond the range of human undertakings. It was at once so simple, so unhurried, so casual, that it was difficult to see it in true proportion. In his cramped cabin, Lindbergh sat listening intently to the steady clamor of the nine black cylinders protruding like a strange necklace about the pointed nose of the plane. The regular thrum filled the gray morning. The light increased. They could distinguish his face at the windows; he was smiling and looking over their heads into the east. East and north Paris awaited, its gray old buildings in sunlight. East and north, and more more than 3000 miles away, by the course he would follow. What he thought during these minutes no one could guess. Fastened to a cross-rod were two canteens of drinking water; close at hand were five sandwiches. The *Spirit of St. Louis* surely was an appropriate name for this silver man-made bird about to take wing for the city that once was home of the saintly king. A proud name to bear, and proudly confident, ship and pilot looked. Slowly Lindbergh raised his hand.

" So long," he said. Casual American phrase of parting. To us, who use it, the meaning is quite distinct. It is different from *au revoir* or *auf Wiedersehen*. It means subconsciously: " I'm going *now;* but I'll see you in a *short* time."

" So long," Lindbergh said.

He opened the throttle steadily. No movement of hurry or excitement marked his going. The plane lumbered slowly forward. Gradually its speed increased. In a few seconds the tail came off the ground. Now there was no turning back. Down the long sodden runway, rapidly shortening, it was difficult to gain flying speed. The heavy load of gas and oil forced the wheels deep into the soft ground. Spectators began to tremble. "Get her off," pilots whispered. "Get her up now, or you never will." And he did. At the last possible moment. Over all obstructions the *Spirit of St. Louis* flew. A moment later the silver plane was out of sight.

All day Lindbergh followed the coast line and at Cape Breton turned eastward over the Atlantic. Rain and fog met him, wild torrents of rain and belts of blinding fog. East he flew through the long night and at dawn was more than half-way across. There was no error in his calculations; no faltering of plane or motor. The sun moved overhead and began to descend. He should be near Ireland. Then he saw the fishing fleet. He dove toward them and shouted: "Is this the right way to Ireland?" but they could not hear his voice. Shortly after he saw the land. When night came again he was following the silver Seine.

Half of the population of Paris was at Le Bourget Field, the other half was trying to get there. By train, bus, motors, bicycles, taxies, on foot they swept in converging rivers of men, women, and children, toward the famous airdrome. Search-lights whirled across the sky seeking the lone American Flyer; beacons glittered a frantic welcome; rockets shot wildly into the dark and burst in a thousand guiding stars. On the peak of the Eiffel Tower were lights in case he was off his course. In the night there was the sound of a motor.

Circling, the silver monoplane sought a space free from the roaring crowds; circling, banking, propeller idling; a short steep glide and a quick landing, and Lindbergh had come.

TO THE LAND OF THE DOUBLE EAGLE

CLARENCE D. CHAMBERLAIN AND CHARLES A. LEVINE IN THE
"COLUMBIA"

From Roosevelt Field, L. I., to Eisleben, Germany . . . Distance 3911 miles . . . Flying time 42 hours 30 minutes . . . June 5–7, 1927.

CLARENCE CHAMBERLAIN was a gypsy flyer. He wandered through the clouds and dropped down wherever he thought there was a chance to take up a few passengers and make sufficient money to buy gasoline for another cross-country flight. Lean, brown, capable, trained at Kelly Field, he barnstormed the country, and like so many pilots dreamed of the one great flight that would make his name, end the arduous and dangerous stunting at country-fairs, and release him to help in the task of advancing aviation.

He was a crack pilot. "I believe he could fly a sewing-machine," one aviator said. Unlike most of the band of gypsy flyers who were left by the ending of the war bound to the lure of the air, Chamberlain had very definite ideas for his future. He was not an "air bum" seeking a little money and a lot of thrills. Deeply, sincerely, he believed in aviation; in great air-liners following regular schedules with passenger and freight, but particularly in the development of a small, safe two-seater for the man who now drives an automobile and who will some day fly a plane.

A year or two after the war, Chamberlain met Giuseppe Bellanca. The extraordinary little Italian was one of the best —and probably the most unfortunate—designers of airplanes in the country. The few ships he had built incorporated features of design immediately seized upon by other engineers. His planes had a maximum lifting power and an ability to fly long distances possessed by few craft. Yet he was unable to become established and was pursued by misfortune and lack of capital. Chamberlain flew a Bellanca and was captivated by its ability. Five years passed. Bellanca had succeeded in interesting some people with money in his business; among them was Charles A. Levine. Although just thirty years old, Levine was already worth several millions. He became interested in aviation and was made vice-president of the Bellanca firm. Impetuous, arrogant, and with the bad habit of making enemies easily, nevertheless Levine had courage if not judgment.

In May of 1926 Chamberlain and Bert Acosta made an attempt to break the existing endurance record with a stock model Bellanca plane named the *Columbia*. They took off from Roosevelt Field with a full load of gasoline and descended 52 hours later, proud holders of a new world's record. Instantly Levine thought: "If that plane can fly 52 hours it ought to have a good chance at the $25,000 prize for a flight from New York to Paris." With Levine an idea was translated into immediate action. The *Columbia* was entered. The plane was overhauled and made ready for the trial. Everyone was interested to know if Chamberlain or Acosta would be selected as pilot. They were close friends and both expert aviators and eager for the opportunity. No one believed that they would not be the crew of the *Columbia,* as navigator and pilot, whichever was given the major honor of being at the controls. But they did not take Levine into account. He selected Bertaude as navigator. When Acosta heard of this he went to Chamberlain and said: "I'm out. The game is all yours." It was a fine bit of sportsmanship. Chamberlain was announced as the pilot of the *Columbia* and after the unfortunate accident to

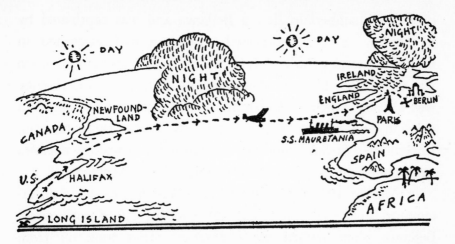

Byrd's plane and the injuring of Floyd Bennett, Acosta was invited to become the chief pilot of the *America*. The *Columbia* was ready to take off, when Levine quarreled with Bertaude and he resigned. Chamberlain was left without a navigator. Press and public condemned Levine for his actions. He was bitterly criticized. Chamberlain said:

"What now? Is it all off?"

"Go on with your plans," Levine answered. "We're not out of it yet."

In the midst of this confusion and bad feeling, Lindbergh arrived, started and finished his flight to fame. Chamberlain was despondent. He believed in the *Columbia*. He knew he could make the leap. This chance he had been working for a long time, and through no fault of his own, he had been compelled to sit idly by and see it slip away. "Well," he said with a sigh, "better luck next time." Levine arrived at the field excited as usual.

"Are you ready to go? " he asked.

" Go where? " said Chamberlain.

"Across, man," said Levine impatiently. "Anywhere."

" What's the use? Lindbergh has done it. It looks like bad manners to follow him. As though we were trying to shine in his limelight."

" How about Germany? " said Levine. " How about starting out and flying until the last drop of gas is gone? Come on, Clarence. Let's give 'em something to shout at."

Instantly Chamberlain was enthusiastic. Lindbergh had flown to Paris; the prize and the glory was his alone. That was fitting. But a non-stop distance flight from New York to Europe was a different matter. It was a sporting proposition.

" Who's going with me? " Chamberlain asked.

" I am," said Levine.

" You? You are? " He was amazed.

" The first passenger to fly to Europe," said Levine. " Everyone has taken a crack at me for what I've done. I'm sick of them. You can fly this bus alone. But I'm going with you."

Bad weather held up the start. On the morning of June 5th the reports came that they could expect fair weather for at least 24 hours.

" Let's go! " said Levine. He and Chamberlain rushed out to the field. The plane was ready, and to the astonishment of the crowd, Levine climbed into the cabin beside Chamberlain. The first start was unsuccessful, but in the second trial, the *Columbia* took off easily and picked up altitude apparently without effort and vanished into the dazzle of the rising sun.

DAWN FOUND THE "COLUMBIA" FLYING OVER GERMANY

North and east they headed on the long grind. The sun moved across the clear sky and dropped into the west. Below, the water looked blue and shallow. The long curved arm of Cape Cod, white sand and small towns, appeared and Chamberlain discovered they were far off their course. He checked the magnetic and earth-induction compasses and found the latter was not functioning correctly. This was a serious difficulty. Lindbergh had been able to strike Ireland within ten miles of where he had planned due to the accuracy of his earth-induction compass. It was the most important instrument in the navigation of planes over water. Its small needle indicated at once by swinging from right or left of the decided course whether the plane was swerving from the true line.

" Shall we go back? " Chamberlain wrote.

" We'll go on to Europe, or to Davy Jones' locker," Levine answered. " I'll never turn back."

Chamberlain nodded agreement.

He put his trust in the magnetic compass, set a new course and pointed the roaring ship across the open sea toward Nova Scotia. The wind shifted into the north, blowing in gusts, and cutting down the speed of the *Columbia.* Chamberlain waited anxiously for the first sign of Nova Scotia. Presently it appeared, dark and clear on the horizon, and he felt easier. His navigation calculations were correct. All the long afternoon they fought the strong headwind. Evening brought the rocky headlands of Newfoundland, and as the twilight deepened they swung out in the great circle, the calm sea was speckled with icebergs, and in that northern latitude, the inevitable fog arose. The night was a succession of clear spaces and banks of cloud and fog. Toward morning Chamberlain began to worry about their position. Fortunately they sighted the *Mauretania* and were able to check their course. Over England the *Columbia* passed, flying high and fast. Across France into the darkness they headed; night brought a gale of wind and rain and weariness for pilot and passenger. Levine flew the plane for a few hours and Chamberlain relaxed from the strain of nearly 40 hours of incessant attention. With the dawn they were over Germany. The gasoline supply was nearing its end. They agreed to keep on until the last drop was gone. At close to six o'clock the motor sputtered and missed.

" That's all," shouted Chamberlain.

Below was a small village and several large clear fields about the outskirts. Chamberlain selected one and brought the plane down just 3905 miles from Roosevelt Field.

Although this was the official end of their flight, they decided to get some fuel and go on to Berlin. They secured a small amount of gasoline and took off. But their luck had deserted them. They became lost and flew south of Berlin. The gas gave out when they were seventy miles from the city and they were forced to land. The field turned out to be soft with rain and the wheels of the *Columbia* mired; the plane pitched forward into its nose snapping the propeller. That was the end. Wearily they climbed out to be met by the astonished villagers.

The flight established a record for non-stop cross-country flying, and Germany and the United States gave passenger and pilot credit due their courage and skill.

FORCED LANDING IN A FOG

COMMANDER RICHARD E. BYRD AND CREW OF THE "AMERICA"

From Roosevelt Field, L. I., to Ver-Sur-Mer, France . . . Distance 3477 miles . . . Flying time 43 hours 21 minutes . . . June 29–30, 1927.

COMMANDER RICHARD BYRD scribbled hastily on a piece of paper and passed it to the crew of the monoplane *America*. They read it impassively, although each of the three realized the potential danger behind the simple phrase.

" Stand by for a landing! "

Curt, decisive, fraught with disaster. A landing? Below them was no bright-turfed airport, no wind-vanes blowing their guidance to safety! No beacons or flood lights to indicate direction or the level surface of the earth, only a row of flares burning fitfully and disclosing patches of black, rolling water. About them the fog still gathered and a cold rain blew fitfully in from the Channel. Bring down a huge land-plane weighing seven or eight tons and flying a mile a minute in water of unknown depth with the pall of a stormy night hiding everything but the line of feeble flares? It had never been done. Byrd knew the solidity of water struck by a plane moving at high speed; the memory of a hundred tragic crashes witnessed during his dodo days at Pensacola flashed across his mind. Again he saw training ships caught in the whirling descent of a tail-spin, hurtling into the blue Florida waters, striking with a force that buckled wings and fuselage, tore motors loose from their beds and crumpled ship and pilot in one inextricable mass. Water yielded scarcely more than cement; it was like fluid iron just beginning to cool. Noville, Acosta and Byrd braced themselves for the shock.

" Stand by for a landing! "

At the controls Bernt Balchen sat motionless as a statue. His face, haggard from forty hours of strain, was set in deep lines. The muscles of his jaw ridged the drawn skin; no movement broke the set contours. Only his eyes were alive. Pale, intent, in their dark, ringed lids they searched for anything that might help him in this desperate climax to a flight filled with unbelievable difficulties. His hands on the control-wheel seemed welded to the hard rubber rim; his feet had become part of the rudder stirrups. A strange sensation of being one with the plane, inseparable, came over him. It was as though he were hurling himself against that black, heaving barrier of water. He brought the ship in at the slowest possible speed and stalled sharply. The tail struck and was torn away; the landing gear was cut as clean as though sheared by a giant knife. There was a tremendous roar and the fuselage threshed in the water like a mad whale. The next few moments left no impression on the minds of the four men. Byrd found himself swimming dazedly alongside the plane. Noville struggled in the water.

" Are you all right? " shouted Byrd.

" You hurt? " shouted Noville.

" No, are you? "

" Are you hurt? " shouted Noville again. " Shot through the cockpit window," he continued. " Right through! " Smash. " Where's Bert? Collar-bone's busted, I think. Are you hurt? Where are we? Just like a sling-shot. Crash, out! Collar-lines cracked. Where's Balchen? "

" Get up on the wing," Byrd shouted.

Noville paid no attention. He clung to the sinking plane and shouted: " The boat! " Care of the rubber life-raft was one of his duties.   With a spasmodic effort he drew himself up on the wing and ignoring his broken collar-bone began to get the raft out of its compartment, built in the top of the plane for just such an emergency.

Byrd scrambled around to the submerged pilot's cockpit and found Balchen entangled in the controls.   Together they managed to free him and he crawled out of the battered plane.

" O. K.? " Balchen shouted to his commander.

" Yes, are you? "

" Are you O. K.? " repeated Balchen, ignoring Byrd's question.

" Where's Bert? " asked Byrd.

As though in reply Acosta appeared swimming on the far side of the plane!   Laboriously they climbed into the wing, the only part of the *America* above water.   Noville, struggling and falling with weariness, and the only one of the crew that had received any injury beyond the shock of the landing, had almost inflated the life-raft.   Acosta and Balchen were asking each other questions at the top of their voices and neither one answered the other.   Then Byrd discovered the three were totally deaf from the thunder of the motors.   He had worn ear-plugs and could hear.   When the raft was ready they embarked and rowed toward the shore.   Two hundred yards brought them into the surf and safely out on a narrow strip of beach.   Wearily, they plodded away in the darkness to find a house.   Presently they reached the lighthouse whose beacon had been their salvation and convinced the keeper they were four Americans who had just flown across the Atlantic.

The story of Richard Evelyn Byrd is proof that romance and

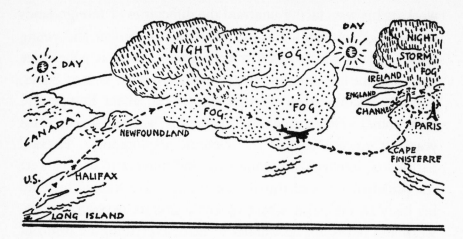

adventure remain in the world. Undoubtedly Byrd would deny that he is either a Romantic or an Adventurer; and he would be quite correct. He is the modern adventurer who has devoted his life, not to the slaying of giants, the search for the Holy Grail, or the Conquering of Nations, but to the conquest of space and time, the discovery of unknown regions of the world we live in, the advancement of man's great invention, the airplane, and the addition of accurate and scientific data concerning the scarcely explored pathways of the skies. The very best type of modern adventurer, his care and daring investigations have added thousands of square miles to our maps, reliable and ingenious instruments to the navigation of aircraft and deathless epics of courage to the chronicles of our age.

The facts of his life have the charm and daring of a character of fiction. When he was twelve years old, he decided to take a trip about the world. He wanted to see distant cities, to discover how men work and think and live, to travel on his own,

working his way, facing unafraid the difficulties of foreign lands
and strange customs.   His mother gave her consent and young
Dick Byrd set out on his first expedition.   He was gone three
years and during this time he traveled across the United States,
over the Pacific, down through the Orient, about Europe and
back home.   He returned, sturdy, self-reliant and fixed in his
yearning toward a life of scientific exploration.   Physical
hardihood, intellectual keenness and indifference to danger were
the principal traits of this boy of fifteen.   He wanted to build
his body to the point where he could endure exposure, strain,
work and hardship; he wanted to learn everything he could of
the new mechanical inventions of men, particularly those related
to the airplane, and navigation, one of the oldest aids to the
conquest of the world; he wanted to go to parts of the earth
unseen by the eyes of men.   The deeds of Peary, Amundsen,
Shackleton, Steffenson and Ellsworth were magic songs, the
fairy tales of to-day.   Hans Andersen and the Brothers Grimm
did not interest young Byrd.   The ogres and giants of their
imaginations were feeble monsters compared to the real giants
of cold and hunger and danger who awaited the intrepid ex-
plorer amid the Arctic ice-pack, beyond the Great Barrier of the
Antarctic, or in the dizzy cloud castles two miles above the
ocean and a thousand miles from land.   These *were* giants to
be slain; regions to be subjugated, Holy Grails to win.   Byrd
was preparing to go forth to battle.   He reasoned the best way
to get the training he needed was to enter the U. S. Naval Acad-
emy.   He was an excellent student and athlete.   Just before
graduation while attempting a very intricate gymnastic stunt he

fell and split the bone of his ankle. It did not heal and when
America entered the war, Byrd, longing to go, was rejected as
unfit for active duty. Confined to a desk job, he resented his
impotence. " If I can't walk," he said, " why can't I fly? "
After many months of pleading, the doctors fastened the split
bone with a galvanized nail and he was sent to Pensacola to become an aviator. At last he was in his natural environment.
Piloting the clumsy, slow training planes he dreamed of the
future and all his desires began to take form. The airplane was
the instrument of to-day. Miles meant nothing to its greedy
propeller; mountains, seas, ice-fields, forests, deserts, all were
powerless to stop its swift passage. But the airplane was not
yet ready for these flights of conquest and Byrd knew scarcely
anything of its art and nothing at all of the new dimension in
which it moved. During these early days spins were alarm-
ingly fatal. Flyers went up and became lost, were never seen
again; aviation needed a more complete technique. New instruments; more reliable motors. The knowledge of flying was
developed by men who died trying to find the way out of the
dizzy spirals of a tail-spin; other men labored over development
of bank-and-turn indicators, delicate altimeters, better compasses, and a quick method of navigating calculations. Byrd
was absorbed by all these problems. He urged that every pilot
should be protected by every possible device. Innovations were
not easily made. The country was at war. Man-power was
cheap. There were greater problems than just the individual
and his survival. No one had much time to consider the two or
three boys who died every day in the cockpits of the training

planes. It was unfortunate, but it was war. "Killed in line of duty!"

Byrd, a competent pilot, a conscientious officer, was put in charge of an airplane station near Halifax. His duty was to patrol the coast in search of German submarines. Several under-sea boats had made audacious raids on shipping in American coastal waters. This task depressed Byrd, who had hoped to be sent to Europe, but it resulted in more opportunity to study fly-ing over water. Then the war ended. The NC planes were being prepared for the flight to Europe. Byrd wanted to go, but his duty in Canada, by a technicality made him ineligible. Nevertheless his investigations of the problem of aerial naviga-tion were of great value to the commanders of the NC flying-boats. He rode with the NC-3 on the first hop from Long Island to Trepassey Bay. The experience was another milestone on the way to fulfillment of his ambition.

Up until this time all of Byrd's plans had been partly frus-trated by circumstances beyond his control. The accident at Annapolis had prevented him taking an active part in the war; his being sent to Canada kept him from being a member of the argosy of the NC planes. One more desire was to be snatched from him, and this time fortunately.

The U. S. Government had purchased a great dirigible from England, and after a final test it was to be flown to this country by a part English, part American crew. Byrd had been trying to interest the Navy in a non-stop solo flight by airplane across the Atlantic with himself as the pilot. The best plane available was still uncertain in performance but Byrd was willing to trust his judgment that he could find a wind current blowing east and secure the necessary cruising radius. The naval heads refused permission but notified Byrd he might become a member of the crew of the ZR-2 on its over-ocean voyage. Jubilant, Byrd caught the first steamer. Preparations for the start of the ZR-2 were almost complete. A last trial flight was to be made before the actual trip. Byrd wanted to go on the trial. Then fate again took a hand. He missed a train. The English commander of the dirigible thought he was not coming. Another officer was given his place. Bitterly disappointed, Byrd saw the silver giant rise proudly and driven by its six motors vanish into the distance. " Just my luck! " he said. It was " just his luck," if he could have known the future, for at dawn the next day the ZR-2 exploded and fell into the Humber River. Only five men out of the crew were saved, and only one of the five was an American. The two nations were appalled. A protest against this waste of life arose on both sides of the water. Byrd said: " We are pioneers. Our business is a dangerous one. Many of us will die but the work must be carried on. The future of aviation cannot be hindered by death and disaster along the way. This is the history of man's progress. The first men who put to sea in boats were overwhelmed and drowned; the first steamboats exploded and killed their crews; the first railroad trains ran off the tracks and many lives were lost; automobiles killed hundreds in the early days; pioneers crossing the plains were slaughtered by the Indians. These men risked their lives to secure safety for thousands to come. We must do the same."

He returned to America, and joined MacMillan on a trip into

AT A MILE-A-MINUTE THE "AMERICA" CRASHED IN THE CHANNEL

the Arctic. The expedition was only relatively successful but Byrd learned many things that were to help on his next venture. And he met Floyd Bennett. The two became friends. Together they planned a flight to the North Pole. Year by year and adventure by adventure, Byrd had been collecting data on distance flying and testing it in the dangerous school of practice.

" We want a three-motored plane," he told Bennett, and he agreed. They selected a tri-motored Fokker monoplane, and christened it the *Josephine Ford* in honor of Edsel Ford's young daughter, for the son of Henry Ford had furnished much of their financial backing.

An expedition was formed and set out for King's Bay, on the Island of Spitzbergen. The pole lay 750 miles away. Men with experience in the North were not too certain about the possibilities of the flight. " If we have to make a forced landing," Byrd said, " we'll walk back. What are our chances? "

" You might make it in two years," these explorers said.

With this alternative facing them, work was pushed ahead. They arrived at Spitzbergen, set up the plane and were ready to try. Bennett was to be Byrd's co-pilot. After three tries the plane took off. They reached the pole, circled it and returned in triumph. Miles of land were seen for the first time; new facts were gathered concerning winds, ice, and navigation.

" Now for the Atlantic," said Byrd.

" I'd like to be one of the crew," Bennett said.

" Wherever I go, you go," Byrd replied.

They had hardly caught up on sleep from the long grind over the northern wilderness.

" Three motors," said Byrd. " Complete radio equipment, a crew of at least three; rations for several weeks, a still for making drinking water from sea water; some form of life-boat and a cargo of respectable size. We're not after a prize; we're not racing anyone. We don't want publicity or fame. This is a pioneer flight in the interest of commercial aviation. Soon great liners of the air will be passing regularly from America to Europe. We are blazing the trail."

Rodman Wanamaker agreed to finance the flight. A new plane was built. When the test flight was made Anthony Fokker, its designer, was at the controls. Floyd Bennett sat in the other pilot's seat. Byrd and Lieutenant George O. Noville stood in the cabin. The great ship took off easily. Every new plane has what aviators call " bugs." These are the unsuspected tendencies of a ship away from normal flight actions. No designer can foresee them. They are discovered by actual flying, and this makes every first test trial dangerous. The *America* had a " bug." When Fokker brought it in for a landing and throttled the motors, immediately the nose dropped. This is disastrous. He opened the throttles and climbed again, trying to find some way of making a safe landing. There was a very limited supply of gas in the tanks. Down they came. The nose dropped, and the plane crashed, the tail whipped up, hung for an instant before the *America* turned over on its back. The men were dragged out of the wreck. Byrd had a broken arm; Noville was internally torn and bruised; Bennett was so badly hurt, his recovery seemed doubtful. Fokker escaped with cuts and bruises. The plane was smashed, but not beyond hope. Repairs were rushed forward, but the days lengthened into weeks before they were ready to go. Then the weather turned bad, storm followed storm. Steamers brought reports of unprecedented gales with winds of cyclonic intensity and tremendous seas. At last on the 24th of June the weather reports were sufficiently favorable to permit a start. The *America* was drawn to the top of an incline at the head of the runway. This was expected to give the plane a greater impetus. Acosta was at the wheel. Beside him sat Balchen. Noville crouched with his hand on the dump-valve ready to empty the huge 1200 gallon tank of gasoline in case of an emergency. Byrd gave the signal. With a rush they tore down the incline. In 48 seconds the *America* rose from the ground. The heavy ship climbed amazingly. On the first turn they actually gained altitude. They were delighted. Although the start had been in a drizzle of rain, they shortly drove into clear weather. They reached Newfoundland, and began to climb, seeking the tail-wind that Byrd believed blew from east to west. The three motors were exceeding the estimated gas consumption, and the commander was worried. If the wind didn't develop, they would not reach the other side. Fog added to their worries. Off the Grand Banks, the dense clouds of fog, rain and sleet enwrapped the plane. There was no way out. Up they went to the limit of the *America's* climbing power. Eight, nine, ten thousand feet and the fog never broke. Down they came almost into the sea, without finding a rift.

Blindly they forged ahead, unable to see the wing tips. The strain was exhausting. Eyes intently fixed on the phosphorescent dials of the instruments they fought on hour by hour through the night. Day came but there was no change. Now the fog was a pale curtain swaying before them. It was worse than during the night. It seemed as though they ought to be able to see; it was lighter but that only added to the deception. All day they flew navigating by the regular compass, and the earth-induction compass. Late in the afternoon they saw water, and calculations showed them far south of their course. They gave up their intention of crossing Ireland and headed for Cape Finistere. A radio from Paris said the city was hidden in fog. That was disheartening news. They were tired, now. Their eyes ached, the rims of their eyes burned like fire. Turn by turn they flew the plane, Acosta, Byrd, Balchen. Noville hunched over the radio hoping to hear of a change in the weather. The second night began. It was worse, if possible, than the night before. Fog and darkness. They were over France. Cities lay below them. Powerful beams shone along the airways. Search-lights hunted the night for them. The billion lights of Paris were aglow. Not as much as a spark penetrated the fog. The gasoline gauge was dangerously low. Suddenly Balchen jerked erect and clawed at Byrd's shoulder. There was a glow through the mist.

" Paris," cried Byrd. He wrote a note to Noville, telling him to notify Rodman Wanamaker they were over Paris. Balchen shook his head. They dropped lower and saw a reflection of light in the dark water. The beam came from one of the Channel lighthouses. Disappointed, they decided to make one desperate effort. A new course was laid for Paris. Eastward they hunted the lost city. The three propellers tore angrily at

the limitless miles of fog.   The sharp nose of the ship bored into
the wet, invisible enemy.   Minute by minute, time passed.
Byrd wrote: " Over Paris now."   They stared with aching eyes
and saw nothing.   The dark pressed intolerably upon them.
They had made the last effort and failed.

" Put about for that lighthouse! "   Balchen read and nodded.
After a long time they saw it.   They circled, dropping flares,
hoping against hope to find a patch of beach for a landing.
Only the slow heavy dark waves rolled into the glow of the
flares.   Byrd wrote:

" Stand by for a landing."

Although they had not been able to land at Paris, the flight
had not been a failure.   The perilous voyage had proved the
ability of a large plane and the accuracy of flying by instruments
alone over great distances.   More than 2000 miles of a voyage
had been " flown blind."   They had established the fact of a
wind that blew from west to east at high altitudes even when
there might be a wind blowing directly opposite at sea-level.
They convinced aviators of the reliability of a multi-motored ship
carrying a number of people for trans-ocean flights.   The three
Wright whirlwind engines did not skip a beat on the entire
journey.   The necessity of constant radio communication as an
aid to accurate flying and of the finest instruments—particularly
of an earth-induction compass—was proven.

With this flight the story of the boy of twelve who set out
alone to travel around the world added its most adventurous
chapter.   But the whole story is not complete, more chapters are

to come, probably the most thrilling and dangerous of them all, for at this time, Commander Richard Evelyn Byrd is enduring the grim bleak Antarctic winter, waiting for a chance to fly over the South Pole.

THE THREE MUSKETEERS

CAPTAIN HERMAN KOEHL, MAJOR JAMES C. FITZMAURICE,
BARON GUENTHER VON HUENEFELD IN THE "BREMEN"

*From Baldonnel Airdrome, Ireland, to Greenley Island, Canada.
. . . Distance 2125 miles . . . Flying time 36 hours 30
minutes . . . April 12–13, 1928.*

IN the thick dark that precedes the first light of morning, a small crowd of mechanics, aviators, soldiers, and spectators gathered about a silver-gray monoplane. Its body in the dimness looked vaguely like a whale, if you did not happen to notice the two heavy wings jutting from the lower edge of the fuselage. When you saw the wings the machine became even stranger in appearance, a little like a bird lying on its back on the concrete pavement between the towering masses of two hangars.

The crowd moved uneasily, talking in low voices, conscious of the dangers of the expedition they had come to cheer upon its way. The darkness intensified the feeling of dread. Men peered into the gloom and could not distinguish faces ten feet beyond. What would it be like sitting in a plane, hundreds of miles from safety; only the bitter North Atlantic tumbling its endless cold waves below; stars hidden in fog, all sense of direction lost in an exhausted mind; life depending upon a round dial, dimly glowing before bloodshot eyes, and a tiny wavering needle, at the mercy of mysterious magnetic impulses. Are we flying north to destruction? south to destruction? or west to salvation? Is the compass pointing a true path, or has it been drawn away by the unaccountable variations of hidden magnetic loads? Is there sufficient gasoline? Enough oil in the tanks? Was that sudden, queer rattle the sign of a failing motor? The motor! With a hundred moving bits of steel, the breaking of any one meaning death; or a leak or stoppage of the steady flow of gaso-

line, or a grounded or broken wire in the ignition system? . . .
What kind of men are these who balance life against the uncer-
tainty of a complicated mechanism?

Aviators, who had been in planes when the engine died suddenly, felt, in anticipation, that quick nervous terror.   But there
had been land below them and a better chance of a landing.
What chance in the mid-Atlantic?   None at all.   Soldiers who
had faced death unappalled ten years before, shook their heads
and muttered: "Not for this chap!"   Civilian friends shook
hands with the three men who were to make the attempt and,
secretly, never expected to see them again.   What manner of
men were these three?   Did they remember Coli and Nungesser
in the *White Bird* who vanished in the darkness never to be
heard of again?   Did they think of Hamilton, Minchin and the
Princess Lowenstein-Wertheim?   No plane had flown successfully from East to West.   Those who flew from West to East
had the invincible figures of Lindbergh, Chamberlain and Byrd
to bear them company.   The three men awaiting the Irish dawn
contemplated a record of disaster. . . . What manner of
men? . . .

In the cockpit of the *Bremen,* Captain Herman Koehl sat, a
stolid, chunky German, only his head and strong thick shoulders
visible.   Major Fitzmaurice, youngest of the trio, surrounded by
his friends, said last farewells, with a true, reckless, Irish courage, and the tall, emaciated Baron von Huenefeld, wearing his
inevitable monocle to conceal his sightless eye, arranged food
and supplies in the cramped cabin space behind the pilot's seat.

This flight was the climax to three careers of adventure.   A

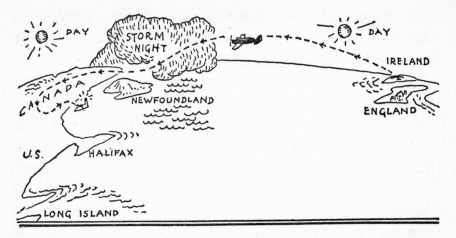

more diverse trio could scarcely be imagined—the phlegmatic Koehl, the vivacious Fitzmaurice, the lean, Prussian nobleman, von Huenefeld—but the same desire to live adventurously, to dare; the same interest and love of flying, bound their dissimilar temperaments with a common bond, changed them from enemies of the late war, to comrades in the present peace.

Each one had, from his youth, a passionate desire to fly. Koehl, a Bavarian, trained to the rôle of a soldier, with a family tradition of arms and war, enlisted in 1914 in the German army. Then he was wounded and while recovering obtained a transfer to the Aviation Corps. Here he served as an observer and later was made echelon leader of a combat flight. It was through his boundless energy that night-flying raids were started, and night-bombing planes developed. He was shot down by two French Nieuport planes but escaped, badly wounded. Three months in the hospital brought about his recovery and he resumed his bombing raids. Again his plane was shot down, this time by anti-aircraft, and again he escaped death, only to be captured after making his way back almost to the German lines. He was a restless prisoner, always determined to escape. Attempt after attempt failed, and not until after the war was over did he manage to get away and return to his homeland.

Germany was chaotic but two or three groups of men were struggling to organize air-lines and Koehl was given the task of establishing night routes. His war experience was of tremendous value; and all the knowledge he acquired as a pilot of night-flying planes was to go toward achieved victory on this most daring of his adventures. . . .

He leaned from the pilot's window of the *Bremen* and waved to Fitzmaurice. It was nearly five o'clock and the east growing rapidly lighter. Ahead of the plane the runway was visible almost to its end. First the ground sloped up a little. Then it descended. A stone fence had been torn down giving additional length into the next field. "Enough," thought Koehl, "but nothing to spare."

Fitzmaurice said a last farewell and walked toward the plane.

He wore the uniform of an officer in the Aviation Corps of the Irish Free State. He, too, was a born adventurer. His career as a soldier—like that of Koehl's—was terminated by a wound. Afterward he transferred to aviation, fulfilling a long ambition, and became a flyer, only to have the Armistice declared before he had a chance to engage in aerial combat. After the war he tried business, but the lure of riding the winds was too strong. He joined the flying forces of the Irish Free State and engaged in many hazardous flights, and barely escaped with his life on several occasions when forced landings were made in rebel country. The previous year he had made an attempt to fly the Atlantic in company with Captain R. H. MacIntosh in a Fokker monoplane. A storm, impossible to surmount, struck them six hundred miles at sea, and they reluctantly gave up the effort and flew back to Ireland. During that season he met Koehl and von Huenefeld who had been forced to abandon a similar attempt. Now he was to share fortune with them in a second trial. . . .

He climbed into the *Bremen* and settled into the right hand pilot seat. The German mechanic grasped the bright metal propeller.

" Switch off," said Koehl in German.

He glanced back at von Huenefeld, crouched in the cramped cabin space.

The Baron signaled his readiness.

He was the commander of the expedition; the man who had sacrificed every penny he possessed for this chance at immortality. And he was the only one of the three who could not fly. Yet the desire was probably stronger in him than in either of the other men. From his boyhood he had lived under physical handicaps that would have discouraged all but a few. Blind in one eye, the vision of the other feeble and distorted, troubled by weak lungs and heart, nevertheless an unquenchable spirit, an indomitable belief in his fatherland and its ideals, an unswerving loyalty to the heritage of " blood and iron " made him a soldier in the war, enabled him to endure the hardships of battle, and, after he was frightfully wounded, gave him the stamina to survive eleven operations so that he might walk again; not only walk but return to the fascination of flying, the whirr of propellers, the scream of landing-wires, the ear-shattering howl of powerful engines. His life was a triumph of a courageous will undaunted by a frail body. . . .

These were the three men, waiting, now in the silver-gray Junkers monoplane, the *Bremen*.

" Contact! " said Koehl, the unimaginative, who would carry on calmly as long as wings and engine could fly.

The motor caught, sputtered, settled to a deep-throated roaring. When that machine-voice stopped they would be in America—or dead.

Chocks were away! The *Bremen* rolled heavily forward. There was no wind. This was a reason for dismay. To take off without a headwind means double the power. A speed of eighty miles an hour was necessary to lift the plane with its two and one-half tons of gasoline into the air. Koehl and Fitzmaurice, side by side, before the dual controls watched the line of little flags marking the runway slip by. In the sluggish air, pressed by its huge burden into the rain-soft earth, the *Bremen* gathered speed very slowly. The slight up-grade was a disadvantage. The needle of the speedometer climbed to fifty miles an hour and hung there. The rise was topped. Now the speed increased. Suddenly Fitzmaurice half rose from his seat and shouted some word. Koehl could see his open mouth but the sound was drowned in the howling exhaust. The Irishman dragged at the controls and the plane, thrown prematurely into the air, rose five or six feet, fell back with a sickening crash, bounced again, swerving and shuddering. Koehl, bewildered

BELOW WAS AN ICEBOUND ISLAND AND A TINY LIGHTHOUSE

by the unexpected action, struggled with the careening plane and forced it under control. He did not know that Fitzmaurice, from his side, had seen a sheep, lying serenely in the path of the machine. To strike it meant a wreck. The only available chance was to hop the cumbersome plane over it. Koehl could not see the sheep. There was no time to think. Fitzmaurice took a chance and the danger was passed. Scarcely a third of the runway remained. Now was the moment of decision. Cut the motor and there would be only a minor crash; hold to the take-off and if the plane did not rise, the flight would end in a heap of twisted metal and three dead men. There was one second to decide! Koehl chose. Squat and heavy, strong sensitive hands clenched upon the wheel, he opened the throttle to the last notch and waited grimly to feel the first sensation of "getting light." A hundred yards from the end, it came. Instantly the wheel came back; not too far, just enough to clear the hedge at the edge of the field. Ahead was a small mountain. The *Bremen* hadn't enough power to cross it. A turn was necessary; a steeply banked turn at a hundred feet altitude, with a sluggish, overloaded plane. A moment to try the nerves of the best pilot. Koehl banked the plane, gave it right rudder, nosed down the infinitesimal angle possible, in order to keep every fraction of speed. It was a perfect maneuver. Not an inch of skidding or side-slipping. Fitzmaurice patted Koehl's shoulder. Only an aviator could realize the danger of that instant; and the superb skill in avoiding disaster.

From then on until dark they had perfect flying. The sea lay calm and bright below them. The light headwind cut only a

mile or two from their speed.   Above, the sun in the clear sky
moved slowly on its huge arc, caught up to them, passed on
ahead, shining back in their faces.   Such good fortune was unbelievable.   They became suspicious of their luck.   There was
something ominous in the tranquil miles.   " It can't last,"
thought Koehl.   " Too good to be true," thought Fitzmaurice.
Baron von Huenefeld, sitting between the two great gas tanks,
caught occasional glimpses of the serene sky and read the notes
passed to him by the pilots.

At intervals of two hours they relieved each other at the controls.   Fitzmaurice, who had slept scarcely at all the previous
night, dozed for a half hour at a stretch.   Koehl caught " cat-
naps."   They checked the gasoline supply and course, and
worried because the flight was so easy.   At five o'clock Koehl,
smiling, wrote a note inviting the others to have tea with him.
They drank hot tea from thermos bottles, flying six hundred feet
above the placid waves, a thousand miles from Baldonnel Field.

Suddenly the sun was gone, and rising before them was a great
wall of fog and storm.   Their premonitions were justified.
Newfoundland, dread region of gales, of wind and sleet and
rain, was sending its advance guard to battle.   Hastily they prepared for the fight.   The wind shifted and blew violently across
the blunt nose of the ship.   They climbed to six thousand feet
and saw still far above them the peaks of the storm cloud.
Night, wrapped in mist and loud with the shrieking wind, rushed
down upon the solitary plane.   The gusts tossed the metal craft
perilously.   They could not relax for a moment.   Now all the
doubts arose to shake their courage.   Was the compass reading

correctly?   They could not tell!   Would the gasoline hold out?
There was no accurate way to check it!   The motor?   The controls?   The oil system?   Fitzmaurice, reaching for his flashlight,
jarred from his grasp, lifted a hand wet and sticky with some
heavy fluid.   He smelled it suspiciously.   Oil?   A leak?   He
scribbled a note to Koehl and showed him his smeared hand.
Even the stolid Captain was shaken for a moment.   They
pumped the gauge level from the reserve supply and in five
minutes it registered only a quarter full!   Again they pumped.
This time it decreased normally and they breathed easier.   The
fog broke and they saw stars overhead and a raging sea beneath.
The storm returned in greater fury.   Now four hundred miles
remained.   The minutes dragged into hours and they longed for
morning.   The fog lifted again and they distinguished queer
patches of dark and light below.   Fitzmaurice fired a Véry light
and they saw the tops of pine trees and a patch of snow-covered
landscape.

Across!

One hazard was accomplished but morning disclosed
another.   The red ball of the sun lighted a country of inde-
scribable desolation.   From horizon to horizon was a space of
snow, ice, forests and bleak mountains.   This, perhaps, was
the wilderness where the *White Bird,* caught in its limitless
barrens, circled and circled until it crashed to its last landing,
hiding forever the fate of its gallant crew.   Unequipped for
travel on foot through this bitter region, a landing meant a
lingering death.   Abruptly Koehl altered the course back
toward the coast.   The gasoline supply was definitely limited

to less than four hours flying. Hallucinations sprang from their tired minds; mirages deceived eyes taxed to the limit. They saw houses, where no house had ever existed; men where no traveler had ever walked. The immensity of the waste-lands frightened them, for born and bred in the thickly inhabited countries of the Old World, they had only a vague idea of the great, empty spaces of northern Canada. The morning passed into afternoon and still no sign of living person in all the snow-covered lands.

Then Fitzmaurice shouted: " A ship! A ship! "

Pointing, Koehl saw what looked like a small steamer caught in an ice-floe. Here, at last, was possible aid. The *Bremen* circled lower.

" *Nein,*" said Koehl, " *es ist ein Leucht-turm.*"

" A lighthouse? " said Fitzmaurice. " Quite so; all the better."

For the first time they relaxed, jubilant.

On the ground dogs ran yelping at the strange bird roaring in the sky. Men came out of the lighthouse and gaped at the apparition. An airplane over Greenly Island? Incredible. They saw it swooping down in the gale, seeking a landing on the ice of the frozen reservoir. Lightly it touched, but the ice was unable to bear the heavy ship. The wheels broke the surface and the plane snapped sharply up on its nose. Then three men clambered stiffly from the silver monoplane. Captain Koehl, Major Fitzmaurice and the gaunt Baron von Huenefeld, crew of the *Bremen.*

The ocean had been crossed from East to West.

ACROSS THE ROOF OF THE WORLD

Captain George H. Wilkins and Lieutenant Carl Ben Eielson

From Point Barrow, Alaska, to Green Harbor, Spitzbergen . . . Distance 2200 miles . . . Flying time 20 hours 20 minutes . . . April 15–16, 1928.

FOR almost twenty hours the slender monoplane had been flying over the desolate Arctic. Now the gasoline supply approached the danger point. Somewhere ahead lay Spitzbergen and safety. The distance was not great, barely two hundred miles and the plane had already covered two thousand; but the dazzling blue, bitter northern day was vanishing into storm. Clouds obscured the horizon, a huge dull curtain stretching across the eastern sky, rising far beyond the climbing limit of the plane. Pilot and navigator examined anxiously the high-piled obstruction across their path. There was still time to turn south and make a landing in Greenland, leave the plane and seek a way out on foot. The year before they had been compelled to make a forced landing, abandon their ship, and travel sixty miles over the Arctic ice-fields. They had arrived at Point Barrow safely, but remembered with regret their biplane left to be wrecked by storm and wind. They didn't want to desert this one.

Lieutenant Carl Ben Eielson, descendant of the Vikings, his numbed feet braced in the stirrups of the rudder-bar, his sinewy strong hand delicately moving the control-stick, stared at the oncoming storm and awaited the final check-up on the gasoline supply from Captain Wilkins, an Australian by birth, commander and navigator of the lonely expedition. Presently a slip of paper was held before his eyes and he read: " Enough for four hours. Let's go on."

Eielson smiled and settled his broad back in the pilot's seat. "Let's go on." How many times had he read those words in one form or another during the last three years? A good many. They were typical of his commander and companion. "Let's go on." Captain Wilkins had learned them on desperate exploration-trips under the Arctic-adventurer, Steffenson. Then they had traveled slowly, laboriously afoot. The snow blinded them, the cold numbed them, the heavy going wrenched their weary muscles; ahead the dog-teams strained at the sledges. In this desperate school where only men with courage and strong bodies survived, Captain Wilkins had been taught the lessons which enabled him to conquer. "Let's go on!"

To Captain Wilkins that slogan was more than an aimless blind plunge; it meant, when the airplane developed, to leave the trudging, heart-breaking methods of the older explorers and utilize the newest of man's inventions. The *Norge* had flown from Spitzbergen, across the North Pole and landed in Alaska; Commander Byrd had hopped off from Spitzbergen, circled the Pole and returned. So Captain Wilkins and his pilot, Eielson, had decided to fly from Point Barrow, Alaska, across the little-known region between Grant's Land and the Pole, and reach Spitzbergen.

Their ship was a Lockheed-Vega monoplane built especially for the flight and driven by a Wright Whirlwind, a nine cylinder radial motor developing 200 H. P. A beautiful airplane to look at, every part carefully stream-lined for greater speed, the fuselage shaped like a huge torpedo and constructed of ply-wood in layers, and pressed into form. A sturdy fast

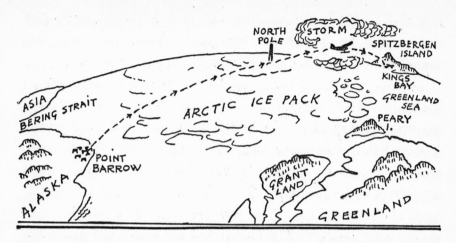

ship, capable of 140 miles per hour, easy to handle, with skiis in place of the customary wheels on the landing-carriage. . . . A good ship and it was proving its mettle.

For twenty hours the motor had roared above the silent empty northlands. There had been no sign of life on the tumbled ice-fields, or in the bright sky about them. They had seen regions never before viewed by modern men. Observations were made, data noted, all adding to our knowledge of the earth. Carl Ben Eielson flew the plane steadily eastward. Captain Wilkins' attention was fastened on the wide barren stretches below them.

Now the flight was almost over, and the Arctic as though roused by their daring, was attacking at the moment when they most needed fair weather and easy flying. Lieutenant Eielson read Wilkins' note: "Let's go on." His lips closed grimly. There was no landing place until they reached Spitzbergen, and any error of calculation might put them so far off their course that they would find themselves with fuel exhausted, over open water. But he trusted his navigator. These two men had shared danger together many times in the past few years.

The first masses of cloud torn by the gale rolled down upon the plane. How insignificant it looked, darting into the murk, hundreds of feet above the world; a slim pointed shape in the dusk, a lonely man-made bird, with a throbbing heart of steel, entirely dependent on a thin, pale fluid that explodes when brought into contact with fire. Eielson's deft hands manipulated the control-stick. The task was one to appall the most experienced aviator. The clouds had not yet closed in solidly. Here and there were openings, narrow paths, splitting and changing while he watched, and along these shifting, momentary, intangible roadways, he guided the plane, an almost superhuman accomplishment, for the speed at which they were traveling and the rapidity with which the clouds altered made his decisions and movements almost simultaneous. The gray dense masses would split disclosing a long descending trail, Eielson would shove the stick forward, the plane would swoop five hundred feet only to have the rift shut and open in another direction, necessitating an abrupt bank and a new course. And all the time he had to keep going in the direction of Spitzbergen.

An hour passed. Captain Wilkins at the windows of the cabin strained to get a glimpse of land. The clouds were thicker and the wind was blowing a gale. Drifts of snow streaked the gray welter. The plane bucked and tossed and Eielson battled grimly with the tempest. The control-stick

IN A BLINDING SNOW-STORM EIELSON SOUGHT A LANDING

jerked against his tired arm. The minutes ticked away and each meant that much less gasoline.

Suddenly Captain Wilkins saw the dark peaks of two mountains protruding through the mist. The pilot had also seen them. He sent the plane down and presently saw a patch of level snow. It might be solid, it might be soft; they had no choice. Eielson braced himself. Close to the ground the snow was so thick he could barely see. He cut the motor, put the plane into a steep glide, pulled back the stick—and they settled lightly, stopped. . . . The flight was ended.

They didn't know exactly where they were, but it didn't matter a great deal, and there was very little to be done about it. They drained the oil, covered the motor and crawled back into the cabin. There were plenty of provisions, pemmican, biscuits, malted milk, chocolate and raisins, and a thermos bottle of hot coffee. They ate contentedly, and after a while went to sleep.

The storm held them five days. They measured their gasoline and found twenty gallons remaining. Then after a desperate struggle, during which Captain Wilkins was twice thrown from the plane, they took off and after crossing a range of low mountains, saw the wireless masts at Green Harbor, where they landed.

The remarkable flight had covered 1300 miles never before seen by man; resulted in much new data concerning prevailing winds, and demonstrated the possibility of navigating accurately in areas where the compass declination is at its maximum.

For this flight Lieutenant Carl Ben Eielson was selected by

American aviators as the leading pilot in this country during 1928. And Captain Wilkins takes his place with the great explorer-adventurers, Byrd, Ellsworth, Amundsen, MacMillan, Steffenson, Peary; men who have conquered the desolate regions on the roof of the world.

FROM THE GOLDEN GATE TO AUSTRALIA

CAPTAIN KINGSFORD-SMITH AND CREW OF "SOUTHERN CROSS"

From Oakland, California, to Sidney, Australia. . . . Distance 7054 miles . . . Flying time 88 hours 30 minutes . . . May 31–June 9, 1928.

WESTWARD into the sunset!
Twenty-four hundred miles from the Golden Gate of San Francisco lay the Hawaiian Islands, romantic upthrusts of volcanic peaks on the wide tumbling wastes of the Pacific Ocean. To reach them by plane was a dare to men and motors; a task equal, or more difficult, than flying from the American continent east to Europe.

Single events destined to be immortal in the record of aviation had taken place in the east but California was becoming slowly the center of flying in the United States. Weather conditions were responsible. There were no months of snow and fog and bitter cold to hold planes idle in their hangars. Landing fields were not deep in snow, or sodden from thawing ice and rain. Pilots on the west coast read the exploits of Lindbergh, Chamberlain and Byrd and looked about for new spaces to conquer.

To Hawaii!

Certainly no man could ask for a more adventurous task. The flight would require the most exact navigation. Miss the Islands by three or four degrees and one would fly on until the gas was gone and fall into the ocean. Tropical storms of unforeseen violence waited across the vast blue stretches of water.

After the Navy flight failed and the PN9-1 had completed its strange cruise, the U. S. Army Aviation Corps decided to sponsor an attempt to reach the Islands. Plans were made with customary military thoroughness. Lieutenants Lester J. Maitland and Albert F. Hegenberger were selected to pilot the great tri-motor Fokker, *Bird of Paradise*—a similar ship to the *America* of Commander Byrd. With clockwork precision the plane was tested, loaded and made ready. The two aviators came to the field, climbed into the cockpit, waved a casual good-bye, and sent the ship scurrying down the long runway. West they headed, at almost the same time as Byrd was watching the coast of Newfoundland recede into the fog.

Hegenberger was an expert navigator and this was fortunate. Their radio failed with usual promptness and half-way to the Islands they were compelled to fall back upon navigation by sextant and compass. Then the motors began to sputter. First one wing engine and then the other kicked and missed, and each irregularity set the hearts of the crew pounding. Mile after mile they covered, tense with anxiety, and each time, just when they had given up hope, the motor would pick up, fire regularly, and enable them to regain a little of the altitude they had lost. Fog and heavy clouds added to their troubles. They climbed slowly to ten thousand feet and broke through into sunlight. Maitland felt happy again. Hegenberger could calculate the course. Below lay a land of clouds, ridged and tumbled, a churning gray country where they had no desire to go.

Peering over, Maitland watched the shifting intangible region and thought: "Here's the place for us. Right up next to the sun. I don't want to go down there again. Now I can see; dipping into that stuff is just like sticking my head into a feather bed. Come along, old lady Fokker. You've got a

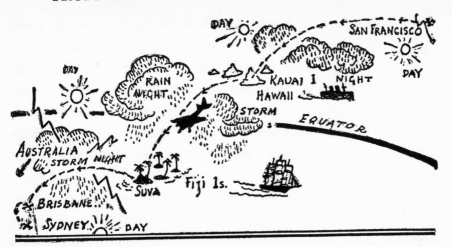

grand voice. I like to hear you howl. It shakes my ears, and deafens me, but it's the most comforting sound I ever heard. Roar it out, you three babies. It's a sweet sound. As long as you holler, we're alive and kicking and going somewhere. To Hawaii! That's where we're going and a square meal. . . ." A gusty, cold cross-wind slapped the plane sideways across the sky. . . . "Hold everything." He grinned cheerfully at his comrade and nodded. Hegenberger, intent upon endless mathematics, smiled back. That map on his lap, covered with figures, absorbed all his attention. They were living by it. Strange to have their lives depend upon a printed chart, several shining instruments, a lead pencil and rows of scribbled numerals. Another gust beat down upon the plane. The great wing tilted wildly and the *Bird of Paradise* rode violently over a series of bumps.

"Somebody pulled the bottom out from under us that time," thought Maitland. "But we've got plenty of space below. I don't like that cross-wind too much. It must be drifting us forty or fifty miles off the path every hour. Cold as the North Pole. Not so good for the motors." He opened the throttle a little to warm the three engines, but they did not respond. The two wing-motors began to miss. A furrow of worry creased the pilot's brow. He touched Hegenberger and pointed down. His companion nodded agreement. There was no choice. The motors were too cold and it was necessary to find a warmer level. Below the gray cloud banks reached across the world. Maitland shoved the stick forward and the huge monoplane began its long toboggan ride. At eight thousand feet they hit the clouds. There was a distinct tremor as they plowed into the denser atmosphere. Then everything vanished. A gray wall moved up and pressed upon the glass wind-shield, swirled around them, damp and chilling, soaking their clothes. Maitland sat with his eyes fixed on the instrument board. The motors were still sputtering; 6000, 5000, the needle marked their swift dive, and the air-speed dial registered 140 miles an hour. It was noticeably warmer. The port engine began to throb regularly and the starboard motor chimmed along. With a sigh of relief Maitland leveled the plane. For a time they flew in the clouds and presently all three engines were running better than at any time since the take-off. Up the plane went, and into the sunlight. Conditions were improving. A tail-wind set in; the engines hummed smoothly; the clouds vanished. On the blue calm sea a steamer moved like a child's toy. They checked their course by it, and found only a slight deviation. Now a darker cloud rested on the horizon. It did not move;

slowly it grew in size and solidity until they could distinguish it for the first of the Islands. Three hours later they landed on Wheeler Field and the Pacific had been crossed.

Shortly after this two civilian pilots, Smith and Bronte, flew successfully over the same route, and out of the Dole Race tragedy two more planes, piloted by Arthur Goebel and Martin Jensen reached the Islands.

While preparations were being made for the start of the Dole Race, two Australian flyers were in San Francisco planning the most ambitious flight yet to start from America.

They were going to fly to Australia. For five years they had discussed the attempt and, now, after endless setbacks it seemed as though it might be accomplished. Efforts were made to have these two pilots, Squadron-Commander Charles E. Kingsford-Smith and Flight-Lieutenant Charles T. P. Ulm, participate in the race. They declined. It was impossible to prepare a plane in the limited time and they were not sacrificing the ultimate success of their long-cherished project by the unnecessary hazards of racing.

The disasters of the Dole Race confirmed the wisdom of their choice. Nine lives were lost. Planes loaded far beyond safety crashed on the take-off; planes not fully tested developed motor trouble and sank into the Pacific; men not experienced in over-water navigation sent their ships astray and were never heard of again. Only two planes reached the Islands. A protest against such a waste of life arose all over the country. No more trans-Pacific flights should be allowed. Calmly, the two Australians went on with their preparations; and the hop from San Francisco to Hawaii was to be the simplest part of the approximately 7500 mile journey.

The unfortunate crashes and losses among the Dole flyers taught them many things. They reached the same conclusion as had Commander Byrd several years before. A tri-motor plane was best for long voyages. They recognized the necessity of a competent navigator and of the best radio equipment. They saw the importance of a type of plane with great lifting capacity and ability to carry heavy loads without structural failure.

" We've got to get the best radio ever put in a plane," Kingsford-Smith said. " And the best operator. We want a navigator who can land us on a pinhead a thousand miles away. We want a Fokker plane and three Wright Whirlwind motors."

They bought the Fokker monoplane which Sir George Wilkins had used in his early Arctic flying; three engines were purchased from the Wright Company; Harry Lyon, a skillful navigator, was asked to join the crew; a special radio set was built and James Warner became radioman. The plane was christened the *Southern Cross* and made ready for the journey.

New delays were encountered. Financial difficulties arose. The months dragged along and not until May of the next year were all the obstacles overcome.

On the morning of May 31st 1928 the *Southern Cross* was wheeled out onto the runway. In the cockpit the two Australian pilots sat comfortably in deep-cushioned wicker chairs;

the two Americans were in the cabin, Warner seated before his radio equipment, Lyon with his navigation instruments and charts. Mist trailed over the harbor and up the steep streets of the city.

There was no bravado about this flight. Waiting for the ground mist to drift away on the rising wind, Kingsford-Smith recalled the long months of struggle, the disappointments, delays and setbacks. The two Australians belonged to that group of zealous believers in the future of aviation. They were pioneers of the air, direct descendants of Langley, the Wright Brothers, Farnam, Bleriot, and Curtiss. They were blazing new trails for the great air lines of the future. Their preparations were made to the last detail. A schedule had been prepared and they were going to keep to it if humanly possible. All their money, all their thoughts and energy, had gone into this flight.

The sunlight straggled through the mist and glinted on the steel cylinders of the three motors. Above their heads the single huge wing, three feet thick and seventy-one feet across, cast its shadow upon the dew-wet earth. On the long fuselage the white letters of the name shone in the early light. *Southern Cross,* brightest and best-known of the constellations of the heavens below the equator. Tropical stars, familiar to those ancient explorers who first steered their clumsy, high-cabined galleons across the uncharted southern seas. Vasco de Gama and Magellan, sturdy, fearless advance guards of the western world, saw these star-clusters glowing like great candles in the soft deep darkness of the warm nights. Closer to them, this roaring bird would traverse for the first time skies which only the gulls had flown. Storms lay awaiting them, tropic rains falling with the density and suddenness of a new cataract spilled from dark cloud ridges; winds of unexpected violence hurtling out of the turbulent cyclone centers of Asian waters.

The mist had cleared. The level pathway lay bare ahead, pointing to adventure. The three motors thundered into life, and the propellers changed to blurs of revolving light. Chocks away! With a shudder the great plane moved slowly forward. Faster now, and faster! The spinning wheels were released from the ground, but continued to whirl as though the ship were ascending an invisible road. West and away!

A long flight divides itself into certain phases. At first there is anxiety. "Is everything all right?" the pilot thinks. "Is the radio going to function properly?" wonders the operator. "Are the compasses correct?" the navigator worries. "What is the drift? The ground speed? The wind direction?" The pilot off duty calculates the gasoline consumption, and puzzles over his figures. "Are the motors eating up forty gallons an hour? That's too much! The gauge may not be registering accurately. Thirty should be plenty at this speed. Twenty-five would be better. How much is left in the wing tanks?" A note is passed from the cabin to the cockpit. "Off radio beacon course, north," and gives the correction. The radio beacon is a constant signal which is thrown directly from the point of departure toward the point of arrival. When the plane is on the course, the sound comes clear and distinct. If the plane moves to right or left the signal fades. The " T " zone is the direction in which the radio note is being sent. The pilot alters his course until the buzz comes in clear and regular. The motors pound upon their ear-drums. Seated side by side the two pilots are unable to hear a shouted word. The first hours pass. Everything is going smoothly. The propellers spin 1600 times a minute. The plane is averaging about 80 miles an hour. The fuel consumption is not above normal. The position of the plane is figured, the course is checked by radio and earth inductor compass and found correct. Everyone relaxes a little. Three thousand feet below the Pacific is blue, unbroken, opaque. The sky above is blue and the sun comfortably warm. Toward sunset cloud banks sweep up from the horizon. White feathery clouds along the top, but growing darker and heavier at the edge of the world. The sun is swallowed and after dusk a wave of darkness falls from the sky blotting out the sea. The exhausts of the motors turn red and long streams of pale blue and yellow trail the plane; flares are dropped to find if the plane is drifting. It is necessary to climb above the thickening clouds. Four thousand feet shows on the altimeter. Cold, up there! Collars of fur flying suits are pulled up over cheeks and chins. The entries in the log book are numb-fingered scrawls. Ulm writes:

11: 36 P. M. P. C. T. Ran into heavy clouds at 4000. Rain. Blind flying.

11: 52 P. M. P. C. T. 4800 feet, climbed above rain and clouds. Stars ahead, moon above.

Now the increasing monotony of the uninterrupted hours

settles upon the flyers. Their ears are deaf but they can feel the continuous thud of the motors in their bodies and are worn and nervous from the endless pounding, the constant vigilance, the inaction. Below them stretches a fantastic world of clouds, mountain-peaks, depthless chasms, miles of rolling hills. Above, the sky is luminous with stars; they look immense, near at hand. The moon streaks with silver the strange regions a thousand feet underneath, and lays in pale bands across the faces of the two pilots. The bitter wind chills their blood, and weariness stiffens their tired muscles. Their "ghost" follows in eternal pursuit, the shadow of the plane leaping across the rifted clouds below. The trail of the exhaust cuts into the darkness. A sensation of passing through eternity weighs their spirits. The roaring miles of emptiness fly out to meet them, sweep by, and are forgotten. There is only a sensation of exhaustion and irritation. Every wish is lost in the desire to have the flight end; to escape the howling engines, to stretch out and sleep in quiet. They sink into a lethargy, performing automatically the actions of lying. The clouds thin slightly. Pale patches of moonlit sea appear. Suddenly Ulm jerks erect, grasps his companion's arm and points down. A cluster of yellow lights moves across the moon path. A steamer! Kingsford-Smith puts the plane into a long glide. They come down to a thousand feet, circle the vessel and send a message in Morse code with their flashlight. The steamer answers. Warner speaks with the radio operator and secures the steamer's position. The brief communication with the world of men makes the crew of the *Southern Cross* feel more cheerful.

Storm followed storm, but the "Southern Cross" roared ahead

The earth still spins below them; they are not lost forever in dark space; men go about their daily tasks on land and sea. An hour later they sight another steamer. . . .

Dawn restored their spirits. The sun rose over a brilliant blue sea. Lumps of white clouds lay like islands afloat on the air. They came down to warmer levels, ate some breakfast, drank coffee, and felt better. Honolulu was almost three hundred miles away. They began to see land, but each time the supposed island turned out to be a cloud. Then they sighted the peak of Mauna Kea and the islands of Mauai and Molokai. Down they came over the streets of Honolulu and swung to rest on Wheeler Field, having covered 2408 miles in 27 hours and 25 minutes. The first hop was completed.

Thirty-one hundred miles south, southeast of Hawaii, the Fiji Islands rest among the eternal foam-circles of their coral reefs. On the island of Suva thousands of natives and every white man were gathered about the Albert Sports Park Oval. Most of them had been there since dawn and now the day was well into mid-afternoon. The natives brilliant in sash and turban of gaudy colors, the traders, merchants and government officials in spotless linen, waited patiently the coming of the *Wanga Vuka,* the bird ship. On a mound apart stood the Governor of the Islands, the Mayor of Suva and their officials. At the end of the little field were a group of ex-war flyers. Fiji Chiefs and their followers from the other islands waited impassively for the arrival of a bird ship that carried men over thousands of miles of trackless water, a fabulous thing the like of which they had never seen. A tall broad-shouldered native was talking in a low voice to his companions.

"Last night we saw it," he said. "The *Wanda Vuka* came over our home in the night. We had been out watching. The white Sahib told us to keep watch and we sat in the moonlight looking up into the sky. Then it came and stood still above us. But it was too early and could not see to come down. It went up to the moon and threw out its great hooks and hung there. And the moon was dark under the shadows of the two great wings of the *Wanda Vuka*."

A murmur of amazement passed over the little group and they gazed respectfully at the speaker who had seen this unheard of sight.

A trader who had listened to the story smiled. There had been a partial eclipse of the moon the previous night and the native imagination had turned this into the shadow of the *Southern Cross,* upon the pale distant planet.

"All night it hung there," continued the speaker. "It was resting and swaying quietly at the end of its great hooks. Then just before morning it went away rapidly."

Further along in the crowd the war flyers stared anxiously at the field and talked briefly among themselves.

"It's too short," said one. "A big ship like that. They've got to come in fast, you know. A devil of a rate. And all that momentum. They'll never be able to stop."

"We couldn't do any more," another said. "It's the only possible place."

"They'll have to pancake."

"That's a sure crack-up. You can't do that with all the weight they carry. No axles or wheels can stand the strain."

They scanned the clear pale blue sky with eyes wearied from constant staring into the sun.

"Just like the old days," said a thin, tanned man, wiping the perspiration from his face. "Remember? Everybody out all in a stew, waiting for the last chap of the patrol. Four ships in and nobody sure what happened to the fifth. 'Went into a mess of fog and clouds over Baupaume,' the Flight-laddie says. 'Came on through. Couldn't see young Searles. Didn't break out this side.' Nervous and worried and trying to look easy. Everybody nervous and worried. Searles second patrol. Remember?"

A pilot who had gotten a little bald and fat after ten years of civilian life, nodded.

"Do I? Good man, Searles. Ready wit, and all that. I remember. Flight-laddie, with the wind up and worried sick. 'Went back in and around,' he said. 'Not a trace. Gas running low so nothing to do but come on in.' All of a sudden Searles' bat-man lets out a yelp. Everybody stretching necks and seeing a Camel wobbling in. Howl and swish and a beautiful pancake with the gear wiped clean away. Out steps young Searles looking a bit shaky and white around the chops, holding his shoulder, but otherwise right chipper. 'Met two Fokkers,' he says. 'Bit of a scrape, you know. Got one with a lucky burst. Saw the poor chap going down on fire. Played around with the other and got this. Just going to finish me off when his motor conked. I came on back. Cheerio,' he says and

faints dead away. Good man Searles. Got his later, pulled out
of a dive and both wings . . ."

A quick shout arose from the crowd. A drone of motors
filled the air, and high in the cobalt blue sky they saw the monoplane. Down it came and circled the field. The thin pilot
began talking out loud.

"Pretty work. Take her around again. You're too far in,
old man. Take —— He's coming down! He can't. He ——
It's a crash, sure. . . ."

Low across the road at the edge of the Park the *Southern
Cross* roared at sixty-five miles an hour. The wheels touched,
the tail skid tore up a long spindril of dust but the speed did
not diminish. The crowd peered, tense and motionless.
Scarcely two hundred feet ahead was a clump of trees.

"He's going to ground-loop," shouted the bald aviator.

"Not possible. She'll go over for certain. Get those people
back."

The great plane thundered down the field. They could see
the flash of sunlight in the goggles on the pilots. Now! The
ground loop was smartly executed. The *Southern Cross* rolled
to rest, its three propellers idly flashing in the brightness. A
cordon of native police kept back the excited crowd.

"I'm too old for that kind of stuff," said the lean ex-war
flyer. "My heart won't stand it. Making a landing like that
after thirty hours in the air. Good men in that bus. Must go
and have a bracer!"

Dawn had barely come on the day previous when the

Southern Cross loaded with 1300 gallons of gasoline had taken off from Barking Sands on the Island of Kauai to start the longest over-water flight ever undertaken by airplane. The three motors roaring, shattered the pale morning shadows, drowned the beat of the surf and brought again the numb ache to the ears of the crew. Up went the monoplane, with its back-breaking load, over the island it swung and headed south over air-trails never before traveled. If the first hop had been uneventful, this one made up for it. They had been out only three hours when the radio stopped working and they were cut off from the world. The closer they came to the equator the worse the weather became. At first rain storms pursued them. They flew around or over. The clouds piled up, hiding the sea, reaching far above the climbing limit of the plane. The rain burst with explosive force upon them. The *Southern Cross* lurched and slid and bucked. In the cabin Warner and Lyon could not stand upright. It took the combined strength of both pilots to hold the plane steady. Mile after mile, hour after hour, they battled their way along. With nightfall the storms grew worse. The rain drove through the joints in the wind-shield and soaked them to the skin. More than half the night they flew blind. The wind shook the plane. The solid torrents beat and tore at them. Morning brought relief but they had used up a great quantity of gas in the struggle. They were faced with the possibility of not reaching Suva. Now the sun shone cheerfully, the radio was working again and they took fresh hope. Far away they saw the outlying islands of the Fiji group. "Dinner in Sidney, Saturday night." Over the lonely green islands they swept down to their landing. They had flown 3138 miles in thirty-four hours and thirty minutes.

The last leg of the journey was barely more than half the distance of the previous flight, but it was the most desperate part of the voyage. Scarcely had the islands dropped from view when the sullen peaks of tropic storm lifted over the sea-rim. A bitter rain poured like a great river from the absolute darkness; lightning ripped and shattered the clouds, the thunder hushed the pounding motors. Beaten, chilled, drenched to the skin the two Australians held the pointed nose of the plane stubbornly on into the dark tempest. Beyond the wind-shield the world dissolved in water and wind and impenetrable gloom. No wilder weather could be conceived. Suddenly a blue flame flickered over the forward motor. Like a ghostly radiance its pale glow reflected on the wet nose of the plane. It was probably an electrical phenomenon caused by the tremendous charges of electricity in the storm, but to the pilots, half-drowned in the cockpit, it was eerie, almost supernatural, as though some strange lost soul had perched upon their plane. Whatever it was, the motors continued to roar and the plane, rocked by the gusts, twisted and tossed about by rain and wind, beat its way forward. Exhausted by the struggle, cold to the bone, their clothes soaked through, the two men dared not take their hands from the controls. During the worst of the storm it took their combined efforts to prevent the ship from being tossed about like a leaf. There was no course; no world lay below them. Only the storm remained, and at its wild dark core the winds shrieked and whirled and clawed the harassed plane; the lightning shattered the gloom with rivers of fire that spread in a hundred, crazy streaks among the clouds; the thunder beat down the sound of the engines and the rain came in a solid wall of water. The night became endless. They forgot there had ever been a day. It seemed as though they had been fighting the storm forever and would continue until they were overwhelmed. The earth inductor compass failed. There was no attempt made to navigate. The two Americans in the cabin clung to the jolting plane. For three hours they flew hoping that the ship was going somewhere in the general direction of Australia. Then the main storm broke into a series of gradually lessening rain squalls until morning brought a gray drizzle and moments of quiet. Lyon succeeded in checking their course and they found they were 270 miles away from Brisbane. They began to watch for land. Presently they saw a dark blur on the misty horizon. Australia! Swinging north, after an hour's flying they saw Brisbane and the iron hangars of Eagle Farm Aerodrome surrounded by 15,000 people. For the last time the *Southern Cross* began its glide earthward, flattened out, and touched in a gentle landing. Deafened and exhausted by the long struggle, the crew of the plane sank back, relaxing for the first time in almost twenty-four hours. The surging crowd broke the police lines and in dark waves surrounded the stationary ship, but the flyers, at first, were too weary to do more than raise a hand in response to the cheers that they could barely hear. The memory of the desperate night still filled their minds, and the throb and roar of the three motors continued to ring in their ears. Presently they clambered stiffly to the ground where they were seized and carried away on the shoulders of the throng. Glancing back they saw the nose and wing of the *Southern Cross* rising out of the tossing human sea. It thrilled them with pride. A worthy ship! Safely it had carried them; they had trusted their lives to it, and it had not failed them.

The last flight completed the 7000 miles, almost completely across water. The plane went on to its final destination at Sidney where the crew were accorded the reception due their courage and hardihood.

THE FIRST LADY OF THE AIR

AMELIA EARHART, WILMER STULTZ AND LOUIS GORDON IN
THE "FRIENDSHIP"

*From Trepassey Bay, Newfoundland, to Burry Port, Wales . . .
Distance 2100 miles . . . Flying time 20 hours 40 minutes
. . . June 17–18, 1928.*

LOG BOOK

Sunday—At the present time we have been out an hour. Land has gone in the haze and we are almost into the fog bank which hangs always off the coast of Newfoundland. We have 1500 feet and both boys are in the cockpit. Me, I am holding down a pile of flying suits as we have left every ounce we could spare at Trepassey and the three cushions were among the things discarded.

We made three tries before we got off and went up from a heavy sea with one motor so wet it had just come in full recently. We had to throw out all our canned gas. We have only 700 gallons with us now.

In the fuselage of the Fokker monoplane *Friendship* a tall slender girl with wide-set clear eyes and close cropped fair hair scribbled in pencil the opening paragraph in a log book destined in less than a day to become a memorable part of the heroic record of the conquest of the air. Forward of the two huge gas tanks, in the cockpit Wilmer Stultz and Louis Gordon sat before the dual controls and coaxed the heavily laden ship slowly up into the hazy air. Behind them Trepassey Bay and the huddle of white houses on the rocky hillside slid rapidly down the slope of the earth, lost distinction in the mist and distance. Ahead in the spaces of the air were 1900 miles of fog and snow and storm, before the coast of Ireland would rise from the sea. Amelia Earhart, the girl bent over her log book, wrote steadily. Already the air was turning colder and she put on the long leather flying coat.

The typical Grand Banks weather rushed to meet the red-orange plane. Fog and whirls of snow; gusts of wind and quick bursts of rain striking like shots on the cockpit window.

Log Book
Bill is nosing her down, all motors wide.

The *Friendship* was a tri-motored Fokker monoplane of the same type of Commander Byrd's *America* and the Australian *Southern Cross*. Pontoons had been put in place of wheels and the long floats hung below the fuselage like two suspended torpedoes. They cut down the speed of the plane but in case of a forced landing at sea might save the lives of the two men and the girl. East the *Friendship* plowed into the gale, the wind shaking the three tons of metal, wood and fabric.

Busy with the log-entries, and the radio code book, Amelia Earhart had no time to remember the other women who had set out on similar adventures. Two of them were never heard of again. Mrs. Grayson's huge amphibian, the *Dawn*, vanished into the sea somewhere beyond Cape Cod. The plane carrying the sixty-year-old Princess Lowenstein-Wertheim flew from England into the western sunset and no trace remained. One other American girl was more fortunate. When the plane bearing Ruth Elder was forced down near the Azores with a broken oil pipe there was a steamer near by and she and the pilot Haldeman were rescued. But there was no time for Amelia Earhart to worry over these past disasters. Ahead the weather cleared. Blue sky above and a calm sea. Stultz at the controls was one

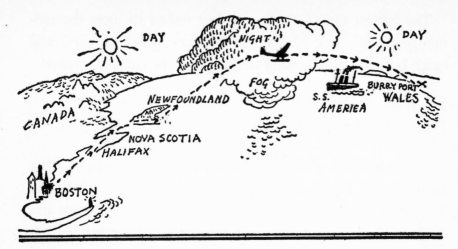

of America's crack pilots, army trained during the war, and later a Navy flyer. He had at one time been a member of the crew of the ill-fated *Dawn* but resigned as he believed the equipment was faulty. He was a trained navigator with several thousand hours of flying under all conditions. Beside him, Lou Gordon, co-pilot and mechanic, had also been a student at Kelly Field.

Log Book
1:40 m. p. h. Wonderful time . . . I see clouds coming. They lie in the horizon like a long shore line.

Quickly the clouds swept down upon the plane. Now they entered a region of white mountain peaks, of tumbling hills, of long waves of cloud. The sea was lost for good. There would be no glimpse of water until they were nearing the end of their journey.

Log Book
     . . . We are sinking in the fog . . .

Kneeling in the cabin beside the chart table the girl could see
the gray world of fog stretching away, limitless, always moving. The last feeble rays of the sun were engulfed in the clouds.
With night the sky above cleared but the clouds and fog filled
the mile between them and the sea. The three motors howled
into the vast space. The air was sharp. Over the left wing tip
the north star glowed. Regularly through the night she made
entries in the book, often writing without a light, guiding her
hand by the margin of the page.

Log Book
     My watch says 3:15. I can see dawn to the left and still a sea
of fog. We are 6000 feet high and more . . .

In the gray light traveling over the unending plain of clouds,
weariness descended upon the crew of the *Friendship*. Slowly
they came down through the sullen layers of fog, hoping to find
a patch of open air, to be able to catch a glimpse of the sea and
get their bearings. They felt they should be close to land. The
orange nose of the plane plunged from the clouds into sunlight.
The sea rolled blue and lazy and 3000 feet below a steamer
plowed its serene passage across the water. They dove and
circled the vessel but their radio was out of order and they could
not communicate. The direction of the steamer puzzled them.
It was crossing their path almost at right angles. Were they
far off their course? Heading south into the open Atlantic?

Motors wide open, the "Friendship" plowed over the rough water

Barely enough gas for an hour's flying remained in the tanks. They wrote a note, tied it to an orange and attempted to drop it on the deck of the steamer. It fell into the sea. A second orange also missed. To secure information was hopeless. They decided to stick to their original direction. The mist closed in again. The ceiling shut down to 500 feet. There were momentary glimpses of sluggish water heaving below; but the fog would close again and nothing remained beyond the tips of the long wing. Minute after minute went by. The patches of sea appeared to be growing larger. Their confidence increased. If the course was correct they would make land. Stultz leaned forward peering intently at the thinning streamers of mist. The heavy plane rode evenly, steadily through the white layers. A quarter hour passed. None of the three moved much. They searched the expanding surface of the ocean for some sign of land. Gordon did not glance at the gasoline gauge. There was no use bothering now. Twenty minutes; twenty-five. Suddenly he tapped Stultz's shoulder and pointed below and to the left. Stultz looked and nodded. A sigh of relief arose inaudible in the pilot's cockpit. Then a fishing-boat slid into the ghostly area below. A good sign. Land could not be far away. Other vessels appeared, sailing leisurely across the misty water. A blue shadow rose ahead. Land? Another illusion? Slim Gordon pointed with a hand that held a half-eaten sandwich. No doubt! It was land! Soon they were over a small town. Factory stacks thrust up out of the mist. Over the harbor there was a lighter area. Stultz banked into the wind and set the plane down lightly on the placid surface, and a gallant girl and two courageous and competent men had crossed the Atlantic.

They stared at the shore but could see no one. Then two men came down, unfastened a rowboat and crossed to the plane. They were taken ashore and the news spread over the world of their safe arrival. But they were not excited. The strain was over; they had arrived, and their tense bodies cried for rest. After a night's sleep, the plane was refueled and they continued on to London, landing on the Thames and completing their intended journey.

THE SILVER GIANTS

MAJOR H. S. SCOTT AND CREW OF THE "R-34"

From East Fortune, Scotland, to Roosevelt Field, N. Y. . . .
Distance 3120 miles . . . Flying time 108 hours . . .
July 2–6, 1919.

DR. HUGO ECKENER AND CREW OF "ZR-3" (LOS ANGELES)
From Friedrichshafen, Germany, to Lakehurst, N. J. . . .
Distance 5066 miles . . . Flying time 81 hours 17 minutes
. . . October 12–15, 1924.

DR. HUGO ECKENER AND CREW OF "GRAF" ZEPPELIN
From Friedrichshafen, Germany, to Lakehurst, N. J. . . .
Distance 6000 miles . . . Flying time 111 hours 30 minutes
. . . October 11–15, 1928.

FROM the enormous dirigible hovering in the bright morning air, a dark, small object dropped. The crowd on the landing-field gasped in horror. For several hundred feet the black shape fell, turning and twisting. People ran shouting and pointing or stood paralyzed by the impending tragedy. Then a long thin white streamer uncoiled from the falling body, burst like the sudden opening of some strange blossom and the parachute floated softly to earth.

In this dramatic fashion Major Pritchard was the first member of the crew of the British dirigible R-34 to touch American soil.

Four days had passed since at 1:30 on the morning of July 2, 1919, the giant airship had risen from its hangar at East Fortune Field, Scotland, and vanished in the fog and night. Four days of anxiety, caused by headwinds and storms that had used up the gasoline supply almost to the last gallon.

For the first time the Atlantic Ocean had been crossed by a dirigible. While the voyage had never developed any unforeseen dangers still it was a triumph for those who believed lighter-than-air craft were the solution of travel by air.

Thirty-one men had made the trip. Ten officers, eleven engineers, six riggers, two radio-operators, Lieutenant-Commander Zachary Lansdowne, an American aviation officer, as official observer for the United States Government, and one stowaway, a former member of the crew who had been ordered to stay behind, but who was determined to go.

Life aboard the great cruiser of the air during the 101 hours of its passage was novel and exciting. Strict discipline was maintained at all times, and the men and officers stood watch and watch in the conventional manner of sailors at sea. Sleeping quarters consisted of hammocks slung along the 18-inch cat-walk that ran inside the ship for 600 feet of its total 670. In the navigating gondola at the bow were the controls, chart room, radio, instruments and two motors. Three other gondolas hung, one on each side and one to the rear, held single motors. Within the duralumin structure of the airship were the huge bags containing two million cubic feet of hydrogen gas; the tanks of gasoline, oil and water. Hot meals were served three times a day, and tea at four in the afternoon. While the quarters were not luxurious, they were as comfortable as possible and the crew had a victrola to cheer them along.

Flying at altitudes from 500 to 5000 feet the R-34 passed over Scotland and out into the Atlantic air lanes. Fog and clouds keep them dodging up and down most of the first day and night. After severe rain storms and fog off Newfoundland, the dirigible passed wide fields of floating ice and saw their first land near Trinity Bay. Above Canada fresh storms were encountered and the trip down the coast of North America was rough and tedious. With gas running low, Major Scott headed the ship eastward and again over the ocean. Here calmer air was found. Clearing weather met them as they sailed above Martha's Vineyard. Barely sufficient gas was left in the tanks to reach Roose-

velt Field on Long Island, and much to their regret the R-34 had
to be landed without flying over New York. The voyage
covered about 3200 miles at an average of only 30 miles an
hour. No attempt had been made for a fast passage. The flight
was wholly experimental, a test of motors and navigation de-
vices, and of the ability of the great ship to withstand all
weather conditions. With the experience of this flight, and a
favoring wind the R-34 returned to England in 75 hours and 13
minutes, just two-thirds of the time taken on the eastward
voyage.

THE LOS ANGELES

The dirigible *Los Angeles* was built in the Zeppelin plant
after the war and purchased by the United States Government
for experimental use. It was twenty feet shorter than the
British R-34, but twenty feet greater in circumference, with
more powerful engines, a higher cruising speed, and a greater
lifting capacity. The interior structures were much alike, since
the R-34 was built from study of a Zeppelin shot down over
England during a raid. Arrangements for crew and passengers
on the ZR-3 (the German designation before the craft was delivered to America) were roomier and more comfortable than
those on the R-34.

On the 12th of October 1921, the dirigible rose proudly from
its hangar at Friedrichshafen and commanded by Dr. Hugo
Eckener, president of the Zeppelin Works, and carrying four
American officers, headed across Germany and France toward

the Bay of Biscay. From Finisterre a course was laid to the Azores and then northwest toward Newfoundland. The huge ship functioned perfectly. Through storm and fog it flew and early on the morning of the 14th reached Newfoundland and turned south along the coast. Mile by mile the dirigible neared its destination. New York was reached and Dr. Eckener flew five vast circles over the city. Whistles and bells shrieked a welcome.

In the early morning, the sun just rising, the silver giant sailed serenely over the tall buildings of lower New York, and turned south over New Jersey to its final destination at the mammoth hangar set among the pine woods at Lakehurst.

The flight of ZR-3 was the longest non-stop trip made up to that time. It covered 5060 miles in 81 hours and 17 minutes, averaging a little more than sixty miles an hour.

After some further tests, the dirigible was officially accepted by the United States Government, christened the *Los Angeles*, and has become a familiar sight on its many flights about the country.

THE GRAF ZEPPELIN

Over the skyscrapers and towers of New York, just as a misty October day was passing in the short twilight, the greatest liner of the air, the LZ-127, familiar as the *Graf* Zeppelin, swung slowly, a shining silver bulk. The drone of five motors reached the crowds in the streets and the thousands leaning from every available window, on roofs and fire-escapes. To the howl of

whistles, the deep roar of sirens on the river shipping, the *Graf* headed toward Lakehurst where the *Los Angeles* seven years before had completed its voyage.

The flight of the *Graf* Zeppelin is one of the epics of air travel. In contrast to the voyages of the R-34 and the *Los Angeles,* this venture was to be a definite commercial undertaking. A full crew of 40 was aboard and in the forward cabin rode twenty passengers making the first trip across the Atlantic. Dr. Hugo Eckener who had brought the *Los Angeles* safely across was in command of this newest and greatest of dirigibles that have borne the name of Count Zeppelin, and this one was to prove to the world his genius and vision.

At 2:00 A. M. on the morning of October 11th the *Graf* Zeppelin was dragged from its hangar at Friedrichshafen. Majestically, the enormous liner swayed at its tethering ropes and as the motors roared into life, tilted slowly, climbed into the rain and mist of a dismal night and started across Europe. The crowds standing on the wet field saw the glowing cabin ports fade into the darkness. Long after the ship had vanished from sight the steady throb of the engines drifted down from the gloom overhead.

From the outset the trip was a desperate struggle with head-winds, storms of terrific violence, fog, rain, sleet and cold. Almost at once it was necessary to alter the plans for the voyage. From the radio-room operators passed the ominous reports of bad weather ahead and in the chart-room navigators plotted new courses and sent their findings to the pilots standing before the intricate apparatus in the forward cabin. The shaded glow of electric lights lit the brass and nickel instruments. Beyond the double row of square slanting windows lay impenetrable dark. The rain slashed across the glass and gusts of wind set the great ship trembling. Low voices conversed in German, orders were sent to the crew at their posts throughout the interior of the vast, pointed cylinder. In the motor-gondolas, engineers and mechanics nursed the five powerful engines and listened intently for any unusual sound. Dr. Eckener moved quietly from chart-room to navigating-cabin, directing the flight. In the kitchen, chefs prepared hot coffee on electric stoves and planned break-fast for the 60 occupants of the huge ship. In the main saloon the passengers sat in comfortable chairs or stood at the windows trying vainly to see into the night. Behind the saloon were their staterooms, five in each side of the passage, waiting to be occupied.

Morning came with the *Graf* Zeppelin headed toward Gibraltar. Now the country could be seen. The day brightened. Farms, villages, towns, rivers and mountains spread out below. Minute figures ran out of the toy houses and waved at the silver giant sailing in the clearing sky. Breakfast was served in the saloon. Conversation became animated. "Where are we?" "There's the Mediterranean!" Everyone rushed to the windows. Blue translucent water, so clear they could see the bottom; red rocks and hills covered with white houses and dusty olive trees. Behind them the high peaks of the Alps Maritime rose above the mist. Fishing-boats scarcely larger than gulls put out in the first breeze. The flat shores of France rose into the bleak, tumbled hills of the Spanish coast. "What city is that?" "Barcelona!" It lay white and gleaming about its harbor. The hundreds of masts looked like toothpicks stuck into the brown hulls of the boats. The streets were filled with people. Now the formidable hump of Gibraltar took form. In the mist the coast of Africa could just be discerned. The *Graf Zeppelin* floated majestically over the guardian rock and the wind blowing from the ocean turned cold and strong. The land vanished. More reports came from the radio-room. Bad weather again. Headwinds; rain and fog hiding the Azores. The dirigible turned further south. Over the island of Madeira a mail-bag attached to a parachute drifted down to the land. The gales followed the great air liner, sweeping it still more to the southward. It was impossible to escape all of them. In mid-Atlantic the rushing storms closed about the craft. Without warning the *Graf* plunged down toward the sea. The floor of the cabin tilted at an angle of 45 degrees. Passengers clung frantically to any available hold. Roaring and shaking the colossus of the air plunged toward the waves at more than a mile a minute. There was a moment of panic. Just as suddenly the ship reared and leaped upward. It seemed as though the frame must buckle, as had the unfortunate *Shenandoah*. The structure groaned and twisted. The wind shrieked, tugging at the ship, threatening to break it in two. Even the deep thunder of the motors was lost in the howling storm. The pilots brought the *Graf* under control. On a level keel the craft rushed again into the battle. Now a report from the rear stations indicated a serious predicament. The wind had torn a great hole in the fabric of the port horizontal fin. Thirty feet of covering had been ripped from the duralumin framework. The gale tore at this opening, threatening to strip all the fabric. Such an accident might render the dirigible unmanageable. The stability of the ship depends upon these fins that project above and below and on each side of the bag just forward of the rear end. In this desperate situation no time was lost. Blankets and canvas were utilized to cover the gap. Four men, one of them Knute Eckener, the Commander's son, clung to the framework and fastened the temporary covering into place. It was a perilous task. A slip meant death in the Atlantic 2000 feet below. The gale beat upon them. The Zeppelin shuddered and rolled like a wounded whale. In the radio-rooms operators were calling all ships within reach to stand by for an emergency. For an hour the fate of the craft hung in the balance. Then the dirigible conquered. At reduced speed, the crippled liner moved on toward Bermuda and across to the American Coast. At 9:45

Down toward the Sea the "Graf" Zeppelin plunged

A. M. Monday the 15th the *Graf* was sighted off Cape Charles. From there it sailed over the Capital, to Baltimore, Philadelphia, and New York. It was a triumphant journey. Planes escorted the huge silver liner. Millions of people gazed in admiration as it swung calmly along through the heavens. City after city gave a welcome to its majesty, to the courage of its crew, and the genius of its builders.

Darkness had fallen when the *Graf* arrived at Lakehurst. Here another crowd had gathered and with difficulty the dirigible was finally landed and drawn into the hangar to rest beside its predecessor, the *Los Angeles*.

Although greater ships are being built, notably the English 101 and two American craft at Dayton, the *Graf* Zeppelin is the largest dirigible in commission. As its number indicates it is the 127th dirigible to be constructed since Count Zeppelin made the plans for the first of the kingly line of airships, twenty-eight years ago. In plan it follows the general characteristics of the Zeppelins. It is 776 feet long, 98 feet in diameter and has a gas capacity of 3,708,043 cubic feet. The motors are built to use liquid fuel—regulation gasoline—or a gaseous fuel—known as Blue gas,—a fuel compounded of a number of gases, carried in special bags and converted into use by special carburetors. The two fuels can be used interchangeably without interrupting the operation of the motor, or making any difference in power. The use of a fuel gas is a great saving in weight and permits a larger load to be carried. The motors can be run either forward or backward without the need of reversing gears.

The cabin arrangements, crew and passenger accommodations, are much superior to any dirigible ever built. While not spacious they provide the maximum of comfort and the electric stoves insure hot food under all conditions.

On its first flight, although battered by continual storms, the *Graf* Zeppelin proved its dependability. It was 111½ hours in the air and covered 6300 miles, establishing new records for distance and endurance.

The return flight to Germany was made during bad weather and without mishap, by way of Newfoundland and the British Isles.

AS LONG AS THE MOTORS LAST

MAJOR CARL SPATZ AND CREW OF THE " QUESTION MARK "

Distance approximately 11,000 miles . . . Flying time 150 hours 40 minutes . . . January 1–7, 1929. Los Angeles, California.

REGINAL L. ROBBINS AND JAMES KELLY IN THE " FORT WORTH "
Distance 12,900 miles . . . Flying time 172 hours 32 minutes . . . May 19–26, 1929. Fort Worth, Texas.

"THERE will be but one objective," said Major General James E. Fechet, chief of the Air Corps, before the flight of the Army Transport *Question Mark*, " and that is to refuel the plane when fuel is needed and keep it in the air until the engines cease to hum."

High in the clear blue sky a great monoplane flies steadily. The drone of its three motors is heard distinctly on the field 3000 feet below. The fuselage and single immense wing is painted red and between the door to the cabin and the rear stabilators are black and gold interrogation marks in place of the large question mark from which the ship took its name. North it goes, turns lazily and returns. On the flying field an army biplane takes off with a rush and climbs steeply until it is above the tri-motored transport.

In the cabin and cockpit of the *Question Mark* the crew takes up position for refueling. Major Carl Spatz, flight commander, mounts the special platform at the rear of the cabin, opens the trap-door in the top of the fuselage, places the wide-mouthed funnel in the pipes leading to the reserve gas tanks and prepares to catch the hose let down from the supply plane. Sergeant Hooe stands by the valves of the gas tanks, alert for any difficulty. Captain Ira Eaker, chief pilot of the big Fokker, is at the controls, his right hand on the throttles of the three engines, his left hand on the wheel. Assistant Pilot Lieutenant Quesada stands in the cockpit to signal the refueling plane.

The third pilot, Lieutenant Halverson, is at hand for any emergency.

The refueling plane passes above to the right. They can see the wheels of the landing gear revolving slowly, the spokes glinting in the sun, and the shadow of its wide wings passes across their faces. From a position slightly ahead of the *Question Mark,* the pilot of the supply ship slips over into the same line of flight and then holds steady, flying a straight, level course. Slowly Captain Eaker brings the huge monoplane up under the smaller ship. Now they are flying level about 30 feet apart and at a speed of 70 miles an hour. From a trap in the supply plane a hose uncoils like a long black snake. Major Spatz catches the end in spite of its threshing and drags it into the plane and holds the nozzle into the mouth of the funnel. It is dangerous business. The air is full of bumps and the two planes do not always ride them in the same way. Captain Eaker watches every flutter of the plane above him, ready to dive, or slip the *Question Mark* to safety. Major Spatz signals for the gasoline to be released. Lieutenant Quesada passes the signal to the crew of the ship overhead. Valves are opened. At the rate of 60 gallons a minute the fluid pours into the tanks of the monoplane. Five, six minutes pass. The tanks are full. The signal to break contact is passed. The planes turn in opposite directions, dive and climb. The supply ship in a climbing turn banks and the crew of the *Question Mark* catch a glimpse of goggled faces peering over at them. Captain Eaker opens the throttle. The big plane regains slowly the altitude lost during the refueling. Everyone relaxes. Lieutenant Que-

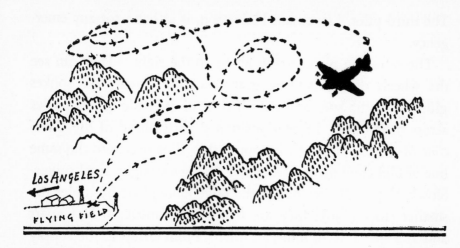

sada takes over the controls, and Captain Eaker stretches out on one of the three bunks. Major Spatz treats the gasoline burns on his hands and then sits comfortably in one of the two wicker chairs in the cabin, entering the data of refueling in the log of the flight.

Just before sundown another supply plane comes up. The same maneuvers are executed. This time packages are let down by rope and received on the endurance ship. In the canvas bags are thermos packs and the containers hold hot soup, hot chicken, coffee and ice cream. Mail is delivered, newspapers. There is a pane of glass to replace the window blown out the night before. The flyers dine comfortably and take up their duties for the night. The motors roar steadily. Darkness covers the earth. They can see the glow of Los Angeles and the lights of Hollywood scattered over the hills. Far to the west a radiance marks Long Beach and the Pacific Ocean. At intervals search-lights from the field pick them up, hold the ship, brilliantly outlined for a moment, and release it to the darkness. Before dawn another refueling contact is made. Oil is lowered in five gallon tins since it is too heavy to flow through the hose. New batteries for the lighting system on the *Question Mark* are delivered, and finally, breakfast, with plenty of hot coffee to dispel the chill of night.

Day followed day and record after record was shattered by the circling ship. First the 60 hours and 7 minutes established by the Belgians on a refueling flight, then the German record of 85 hours, and finally the records of the lighter-than-air craft, the ill-fated French dirigible *Dixmunde,* and the 111 hour flight of the *Graf* Zeppelin.

The *Question Mark* swung into its seventh day aloft. Suspicious sounds were coming from the left wing motor but they decided to refuel again. During the contact the motor stopped and the plane under its heavy load lost 1500 feet altitude. Sergeant Hooe went out on the cat-walk to see if it was possible to repair the engine but a brief examination showed it to be impossible. The right wing motor was going bad, and the motor at the nose of the fuselage was rapidly losing power. Major Spatz gave the order to descend. The gasoline just taken aboard was dumped to lessen the strain of landing, and the *Question Mark* wobbling badly, and with only one engine functioning, came to earth exactly 150 hours 40 minutes and 15 seconds after it had taken off.

During this time it was estimated that the plane had flown over 11,000 miles, or almost half-way around the world. The crew were in excellent physical condition, except for the temporary deafness, and the motors, not worn outside of the rocker arms.

The drone of a distant motor fills the air, and a young cowpuncher riding range over the lonely Texas Panhandle sits erect in his saddle, turns and stares under a shading hand into the bright hot sky. Wings etch a dark line in the brilliance. Presently he can see the plane, flying in its swift passage until it vanishes in the far heavens. Then he sighs, relaxes and rolls a cigarette. Day after day he has watched planes soaring above him; and each time a vague resolution has become more definite.

That evening at the ranch he makes a decision.

"I'm through," he says. "No more cattle for this boy."

"What are you going to do, Jim?"

"I'm going to fly."

There is a roar of laughter from his companions, range riders like himself, the last of a one-time romantic band.

"Cow punchin' is out," says Jim Kelly, grinning. "It's old-fashioned. There's no kick in ridin' the hurricane deck of a bronc any more. Flying's the game. I'm going to get into it."

He packed his duds and departed for an aviation school.

"The next time you see me," he said, "I'll be sittin' pretty ten thousand feet up in the blue, ridin' a horse that can gallop a hundred miles an hour."

"The next time we see you," said the ranch boss, "they'll be filing a motor from around your neck."

"Well," said Jim, "so long!"

"So long, kid. Good luck!"

"You forgot your spurs, Kelly."

"My horse ain't goin' to need spurs."

In another part of the great state of Texas, a motor me-chanic climbed out of a plane and he slung his helmet and goggles furiously into the cockpit. The pilot of the plane snapped:

"You'll never learn to fly!"

"No?" said the passenger.

"Not in a million years!"

"All right. Watch me."

Reg Robbins, the mechanic, smiled and walked away. He bought a second-hand plane and took it out on a barren stretch of country. Hour after hour he taxied across the level fields, getting the feel of the plane, learning the motor. Then he turned the ship into the wind and gave it the gun. Confidently he took off in his solo flight. "Never learn to fly?" he mut-tered. "Who says so! Come around, baby. Easy turn, easy bank; keep the nose down; level her off. Perfect; not a slip or skid. Who says I can't fly? Now, take her in. Nice steady glide; throttled down. Forty-five, just right. Ten feet altitude; level off and let her down easy. Two feet now, and all pretty. Neat stall. Stick all the way back. Just like a feather! Never learn, eh? Let's do it again, baby."

Days of practice; patiently, confidently, taking no foolish chances, learning the air, studying his plane, and motor; cross-

THE HOSE WAS LOWERED AND FUEL TAKEN ABOARD THE "QUESTION MARK"

wind landings, take-offs down wind, coming in on a dead stick; a born flyer.

Robbins bought another plane, a Ryan cabin monoplane, the model developed along the lines of the *Spirit of St. Louis,* and a second-hand Wright Whirlwind motor. In two years he flew 50,000 miles, carried hundreds of passengers and became one of the best known and popular commercial pilots in the Southwest.

He read of the endurance flight of the *Question Mark.* That shouldn't be hard to beat, he thought. Then he met Jim Kelly who had completed his course and received a transport pilot's license. The ex-cowboy was a competent aviator. He was enjoying the thrill of riding his mechanical horse through the air at two miles a minute.

"How would you like to have a shot at the refueling record?" said Robbins.

"When do we start?" Kelly replied.

"Right away!"

They set to work overhauling the plane. Larger gas tanks were installed. A navy hammock was slung over the tanks. From the cabin a cat-walk eight inches wide was built out along the nose so they could reach the motor and make repairs in flight.

"The *Question Mark* had to come down because the valve rocker arms were loose," said Robbins. "We'll see that doesn't happen."

"You ought to get a new motor," friends protested. "How long has that one run?"

"Five hundred hours," said Robbins.

"It won't last. Get a new one."

"That motor I know as well as my right hand," replied Robbins. "I know every squeak and rattle and roar. It's good for two hundred hours, maybe three hundred. I wouldn't trade it for six new ones."

The plane was christened the *Fort Worth* and rose into the air on Sunday, May 19th. Spectators were interested, but dubious. Robbins and Kelly were absolutely confident.

"When we come down," said Robbins, "the record of the *Question Mark* will be smashed into so many pieces that no one will bother to pick it up."

The first day passed successfully. The refueling plane made its first contact and the long grind settled into a routine. Gasoline, oil, supplies, and food were taken on. The early morning and late evening were found best for refueling, as the air was quieter. The *Fort Worth* flew at low altitudes during the day, but at night climbed to 10,000. For the first 48 hours both men suffered from air-sickness, caused by the nervous tension. By the third day they had almost forgotten ever having lived on the earth. Twice a day one of them would venture out on the narrow cat-walk, and grease the rocker arms, and inspect the motor. Hour after hour passed without accident. The weather was relatively pleasant, and they did not suffer from the cold. Plenty of hot food was sent up to them. On Sunday, the 26th, the *Fort Worth* exceeded the 150 hours flown by the red Army transport. Robbins dropped a note and said they expected to go at least 200 hours.

But their luck deserted them. Robbins on one of his visits to the motor, leaned too far out, and the propeller struck the buckle on his safety belt. The blow was sufficient to crack the propeller slightly. That night the ship ran into a hail storm and the propeller was damaged more seriously. The crack spread and the vibration increased to a dangerous degree. The *Fort Worth* had been 172 hours 31 minutes and 10 seconds in the air. Lazily the monoplane turned over the field, came slowly in and the flight was over.

All records of lighter or heavier-than-air crafts had been smashed by this single motored, rebuilt plane, flown by a cowboy and a mechanic who could " never learn to fly."

Even this record was soon to be eclipsed. On June 30 Sergeants Roy Mitchell and Byron Newcomb added two hours to the refueling flight time and then Loren Mendell and R. B. Reinhart, two " tough hombres " as they claimed to be, kept their second-hand plane, the *Angeleno,* aloft for the amazing record of 246 hours and 43 minutes. It is estimated they traveled almost 20,000 miles, or four-fifths of the circumference of the earth. Both pilots and motor were in good condition and only the tearing loose of a section of fuselage fabric which fouled the rudder forced them to land. During the flight they used 4,085 gallons of gasoline, 105 gallons of oil and averaged 80 miles an hour.

Scarcely had the *Angeleno* landed when new reports began to come in from St. Louis where Dale Jackson and Forest O'Brine in the *St. Louis Robin* were pursuing a monotonous, circular route far above the airport. Hour by hour they continued. The mark of the *Angeleno* was reached and passed and notes dropped indicated the pilots would attempt to reach three hundred hours. Steadily the bright red plane covered the miles. Refueling went on at regular intervals without incident. The crew cleaned and oiled the motor. At the three hundred hour mark they made no move to descend. Day after day passed. Finally, after entering the eighteenth day, and reaching four hundred hours, they were requested to descend. Although plane and motor still functioned, the *Robin* was brought back to earth after establishing the incredible record of four hundred twenty hours and fifteen minutes.

CAPTAIN HAWKES COMES EAST

Captain Frank E. Hawkes and Oscar Grubb

From Los Angeles, California, to Roosevelt Field, L. I. . . . Distance 2700 miles . . . Flying time 18 hours 21 minutes . . . February 4–5, 1929.

MIDNIGHT!

Three miles above the silent pueblos of New Mexico a monoplane with a dark red fuselage and a silver wing is hurtling east at 150 miles an hour. The motor thunders its song through the cold, lonely darkness. The stars in the clear sky above appear of enormous size. The scarlet flame from the exhaust sweeps back in a pennon of fire. The man-made comet dragging its glowing tail rushes toward the distant Atlantic. In the open cockpit the pilot wrapped in a fur coat, hooded and goggled, studies the instrument board, moves the stick gently as the wind lurches the plane, and listens to the deep roaring of the motor. Forward, in the cabin, the mechanic, wedged in among 50 or 60 five-gallon tins of gasoline, pumps steadily, forcing the precious fluid up into the wing-tanks where it will flow into the motor.

The world below is blotted out by clouds that lay in a blanket 10,000 feet thick. Since ten o'clock no trace of the earth has appeared; not a light, not a glimpse of a mountain peak; only the pale rolling smother lit by the wan light from the stars.

The clock on the board shows midnight.

Without warning the motor gasps, chokes and dies. The howling rush of the wind sweeps down upon the astounded pilot. He switches on to the feed line from the left wing-tank. The motor roars into action; the plane is alive again. The pilot draws a deep breath. The next instant the motor once more stops. A whirl of ideas flashes across the pilot's mind. . . .

" Finished. No chance to land. Fast ship. Dark. Fog, rain, storm; unknown country. Absolutely sure crash. Three hundred gallons of gas on board in loose tins. Crash and fire. The plane ablaze instantly. A great flaming torch. Over the side. At 15,000 feet. Plenty of time. Mechanic first. Hard for him to get out. Tough. Never left a ship before. Brand new plane. Won't be worth a nickel. Nothing left but a heap of twisted metal. Over we go! One question first! . . ."

The pilot shouted into the cabin:

" What's wrong in there? "

The mechanic was bent over pumping desperately. As suddenly as it had stopped, the motor caught again, crashed in regular rhythm. The plane swung on. The pilot sighed and wiped his face. The whole affair had taken barely thirty seconds. He felt as though he had been a lifetime suspended in the midnight sky, behind the dead motor.

Soldier of fortune in the air, Captain F. M. Hawkes had had few moments to compare with that one. The failure of the motor would have meant the loss of the ship and the end of his effort to break the transcontinental record of 18 hours 58 minutes made by Col. Arthur Goebel in the famous and ill-fated *Yankee Doodle,* the year before. Thinking of his narrow escape, Captain Hawkes remembered the finish of the pure white monoplane which had cut almost nine hours from the time set by Macready and Kelly in the T–2 Fokker. Under just such conditions the *Yankee Doodle* had made its last flight; and not such a long distance away. On a night of fog and rain the motor had begun to miss. A landing was necessary. The pilots

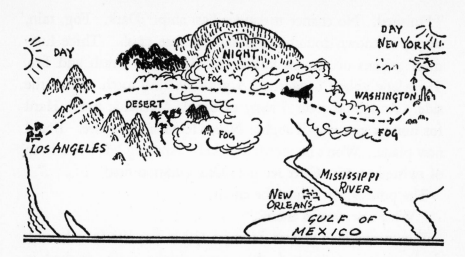

came down seeking frantically for a break in the murk; fifty feet, twenty-five, just enough to give them a chance to flatten out before the crash! Fate was against them. The *Yankee Doodle* smashed on the wall of a canyon, exploded and fell in a burning tangle. On a night like this. The chances of the game. Night flying was always dangerous, particularly over the mountains where a forced landing resulted inevitably in a crack-up. "Stay up high," thought Hawkes. "Give yourself plenty of space and the chances are in your favor."

He was glad it had not been necessary to take to their parachutes and leave the plane to plunge down to complete ruin. Shifting his course to allow for a slight side wind he resumed his vigilance. In the cabin, Oscar Grubb, the mechanician, pumped the gas from the cans into the tanks; cut the empty five gallon tins into strips with a pair of shears and spread the flattened tins upon the floor. Gradually he had room to move more than his arms. The fumes of gasoline filled the cabin and made him ill. The cold was intense. His hands became numb and two fingers were frozen. The roar of the motor beat at his brain until he was sick and dizzy. All night he pumped and all night the dark red Lockheed—" Air-Express " swept over the dense clouds at 140, 150, 160 miles an hour.

At 5:30 on the afternoon of February 4th Captain Hawkes had waved his hand. Chocks were jerked from under the wheels and his plane shot down the runway. It lifted easily considering its heavy load and as darkness fell it was climbing steadily up the San Bernardino Valley. On either side the mountains rose in height upon height. Hawkes followed the blinking signal-lights of the air-mail route and crossed the mile-high summit with plenty of altitude to spare. The plateau of Arizona was hidden in darkness and the red monoplane flashed east across the desert, ascending, still higher. There was to be a bonfire burning as a guide at Clifton but he could not distinguish it. He had climbed the plane to 15,000 and decided to hold that altitude during the night. Another fire was to be burning at Roswell, New Mexico. Long before the plane was on the spot, he could see the wavering flames almost three miles below. The clouds began forming between the plane and the earth. A huge bank gathered, rising almost to 10,000 feet. Now he had to depend upon compass and dead reckoning to keep his course, a difficult task in a plane going two and a half miles a minute. The hours passed, midnight came with its near disaster. On they went into the rising sun. Upon the

Over desert and mountain the "Yankee Doodle" went to a new record

layers of cloud the sun reflected in a blinding radiance. Hawkes brought his ship down until it seemed as though the wheels were running over the fleecy crests. He was beginning to worry. Where was he? Over Indiana by his calculations, but he couldn't be certain. There was nothing to do but dip into the clouds and go down, hoping they did not extend clear to the ground. Foot by foot the plane descended. At 100 feet altitude the mist and fog was filled with a blinding snow. At fifty feet the plane shot into the open. It was a miserable view the pilot gazed upon. A whirling snow-storm blew across the rugged, unknown country. Not a house, no landmark of any kind told him where he might be. For a half hour he risked a bad crash hunting for some recognizable spot. Realizing there was little chance he climbed back above the storm and flew on, as he hoped, in the general direction of New York. An hour later he again drove the ship through the storm and found himself near Washington. The weather began to clear. He opened the throttle wide as the silver-winged plane hurtled along at three miles a minute. New York came into view and then Roosevelt Field. A little group of people awaited in the cold midwinter afternoon. A speck appeared in the west. Driving at 200 miles an hour came the plane. Passed with a roar; over in a vertical bank, the great wing glittering. Twice around the field he went, turning the ship on its wing tip, and in a last rushing glide came down in a perfect three point landing. The record was broken.

In the early summer Captain Hawkes, not content with his remarkable flight, decided to attempt a round trip to the coast and back to New York. Flying a Lockheed *Express* monoplane, he took off from Roosevelt Field and hurtled westward. High in the night he flew, three miles above the earth, arriving at Los Angeles eight hours under the record. He had planned to rest only two or three hours, but the motor needed adjustments and he did not get away for the return flight until seven hours later. Fast as his first west-east trip had been, this one was faster. Minute by minute, he clipped the old record. Alone, with only a brief rest after his outward trip, he sped toward New York. Down he came, completing the two-way flight in a little over 36 hours. Landing, the plane went somewhat out of control, over-ran the field and crashed into a wire fence, but the intrepid captain climbed, grinning and unhurt, from the cockpit of his plane.

SONS OF THE TRICOLOR

Armano Lotti, Jr., Jean Assollant and Rene Lefevre
in the "Yellow Bird"

*From Old Orchard Beach, Maine, to Comillas, Spain . . .
Distance 3400 miles . . . Flying time 30 hours 17 minutes
. . . June 14–15, 1929.*

SONS OF THE TRICOLOR

TWENTY years ago a burly little Frenchman climbed into the cockpit of a strange looking airplane. Dawn was just breaking and in the pale light the machine looked too frail to carry the weight of a man. Only the portion of the fuselage where the pilot sat was enclosed, the rest was an open framework of fragile longerons and cross rods. The two stubby wide wings projected from the lower edge of the body and a tiny three-cylinder motor of twenty-five horse power sputtered and kicked in the chill morning air. The monoplane rested on three bicycle wheels and the wings were braced with an intricate arrangement of wires. Presently the motor began firing steadily and the pilot, Louis Blériot adjusted his goggles and waved to the mechanics to release their hold.

The small plane bounced forward and the few spectators watched tensely. Into the air the machine rose, gaining height so slowly they expected to see it crash on the high dunes that border the English Channel near Calais, or become entangled in the wires of a telegraph line along the shore. But the pilot knew his ship—he had flown twenty-five miles in it only a short time before, an unprecedented distance—and he cleared all obstructions and headed toward the Channel on the first overwater flight in an airplane.

A half hour later he landed near a French flag placed to guide him, in a field near Dover. The landing was a bad one, but the pilot was unhurt.

A Frenchman had flown the Channel!

Eighteen years later two Frenchmen prepared for another over-water flight, this time the Atlantic Ocean. Picturesque and gallant men were the crew of *The White Bird*. Charles Nungesser, the " Prince of Pilots " one of the few survivors of the great fighting-men of the French air force. He had a record of forty-five German planes shot down in combat. Every decoration possible to bestow had been given him. Wounded times without number, his knee, his elbow and jaw replaced with aluminum joints, this gallant son of the tricolor planned his greatest battle for " The Glory of France." His companion and navigator was scarcely less renowned. Francois Coli had but one eye, the other had been lost in the war. He, too, wore the Cross of the Legion of Honor.

Up they went escorted by four planes. Westward *The White Bird* thundered. " We will land by the Statue of Liberty," said Nungesser. They were never seen or heard of again. Birdmen of the Tricolor! For the Glory of France!

Two years passed.

When the spring weather began to break the grip of the northern winter, dissipate the fogs of Newfoundland, and quiet the turbulent storms, three young Frenchmen prepared to fly from America to Paris, for the glory of France and in memory of Nungesser, Coli and *The White Bird*.

Originally the start was to be made from Long Island, but tests proved it to be uncertain if the great yellow monoplane, a Bernard 191, could rise with enough fuel to make a possible voyage to Paris. They decided to take off from Old Orchard

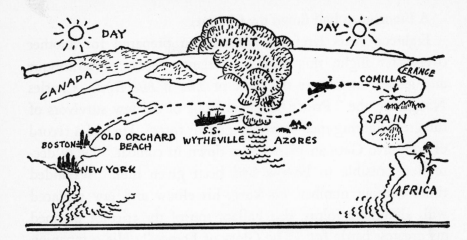

Beach in Maine, and flew north. Along with them went an American airplane the *Green Flash,* a Bellanca monoplane, piloted by Rodger Q. Williams and Lewis A. Yancey. The Americans were attempting a flight to Rome. The two planes were going to fly part of the way together. Bad weather set in and delayed the start. Finally on May 29, the reports indicated possible success. The two huge ships were loaded with fuel, the motors given a final inspection. The *Green Flash* started first. Down the wet, hard sand it roared. Suddenly it swerved, ground-looped and stopped with the left wheel buried. Fortunately the flyers had dumped their gasoline and the plane was not strained.

The *Yellow Bird* barely escaped a worse fate. It rose sluggishly but could not clear a steel amusement pier. A turn was necessary. Grimly young Jean Assollant banked the overladen ship. A burst of spray shot up where one wheel cut the crest from a wave. Slowly the plane lifted and headed out to sea;

vanished in the mist, while the American aviators rushed the refueling of their craft for a second effort. Before they were ready, the drone of a motor could be heard. Presently the astonished watchers saw the French ship returning. It glided swiftly down to a perfect landing. The crew stepped sadly from the cabin.

" A leak in the gasoline line," said Lotti, briefly.

The weather became unsettled. Storm followed storm and not until June 14th, the tenth anniversary of the first crossing of the Atlantic by Alcock and Brown, did the flyers receive any reassuring news from the office of Dr. James H. Kimball, the little man who has plotted all the weather forecasts for trans-Atlantic flights since Lindbergh's heroic passage.

Again the two ships were wheeled onto the flying line. The misfortune of the first attempt was repeated with the *Green Flash* only with more disastrous results. The plane went out of control, ground-looped, smashing the under-carriage, the propeller, damaging the motor and cracking the fuselage just forward of the tail. The two Americans were unhurt but the machine was wrecked beyond hope of repair.

In the cabin of the *Yellow Bird* the three French aviators prepared for their attempt. Assollant was at the controls. Overhead a U. S. Coast Guard amphibian circled waiting to act as escort. Looking down the observer could see the long beach, dark and wet, the lines of white breakers rolling in, the wide bright wings, shining nose and the red, white and blue stripes of the tricolor athwart the fuselage. The crowd about the plane surged back. Tiny figures tugged upon the long propeller. It blurred in a whirl of light as the mechanics sprang out of the way. The observer touched his pilot and pointed. The *Yellow Bird* moved slowly forward. Although its speed increased to a mile a minute it scarcely seemed to move. On it went, rushing up the hard sands. The observer watched it closely. He saw the shadow of the plane leap to one side and knew the wheels were off the ground. He slapped the pilot twice.

"Swell chap, that Frenchie," he bellowed. "Knows his stuff."

The *Yellow Bird* was rising reluctantly. It cleared the pier and after a time risked a turn; made it safely and pointed east. The observer shook his head.

"I wonder why he don't come up a little," he thought. "Can't he climb any higher? He's too close with all that load on board."

The Coast Guard amphibian banked and flew above and to the rear of the French plane. For twenty minutes they sped and the *Yellow Bird* had scarcely gained any altitude. The observer was worried and motioned to the pilot, shaking his head, and indicating the danger of the plane below. The pilot shrugged, but he gave more attention to the other ship than to his own.

On board the *Yellow Bird,* the crew were equally worried by the sluggishness of their craft. The huge six hundred horse-power Hispano-Suiza motor was roaring full out, but the plane would not lift. At the controls Assollant fretted, with a dark line of perplexity between his eyes. The ship kept sagging

by the tail. He couldn't understand why. It had never acted
in that manner before. He motioned to Rene Lefevre, the
navigator, and indicated the constant movement of the controls
necessary to counteract the heaviness in the stern. Lefevre
shook his head. He had felt it and could not think of any
reason.

Armano Lotti was busy adjusting the radio preparatory to
sending out the first message of the flight when to his amazement he saw the figure of a man crawling out of the dark tail
of the fuselage. He rubbed his eyes, unable to believe what
he saw, but there was no doubt of it. A thin, pale young man
looking very disheveled and unhappy crouched behind him,
his hands outstretched in a gesture of explanation. Lotti
jerked at the shoulders of his two companions, they turned and
at the sight of the unwelcome passenger, their mouths dropped
open and blank bewilderment shone in their eyes. Their sur-
prise turned to anger.

" What are you doing here? " shouted Lotti.

The passenger shook his head. He could not understand
French.

Assollant now realized why it had been so difficult to keep
the tail up during their take-off and why the *Yellow Bird* gained
altitude so slowly. In a long distance flight weight is calculated
to the pound and here was 130 or 140 pounds they had not
counted on. The three Frenchmen were furious, but they were
true sportsmen.

" We'll go on," said Lotti. " Let him come. If we turn
back the people may think it is just an excuse. We will have

The escort plane waved farewell and the "Yellow Bird" swung eastward

to dump all the gas to make a landing without straining the ship, and then there is everything to do over again with the chance of a crash on the take-off."

Assollant and Lefevre agreed. With the stowaway up forward the plane handled easier. It began to climb slowly. Better to keep on! The addition of the fourth person was a desperate handicap, but having made their decision they began to plan the best thing to do. The motor of the *Yellow Bird* had to be kept running at top speed. There was no margin of safety now. Gasoline was being consumed far beyond the rate they had calculated. Already they began to suspect that there was little chance of reaching Paris; they shut the idea from their minds and concentrated grimly on getting across the ocean.

The stowaway was a young fellow who lived in Portland, Maine. Unseen, he had entered the cabin of the plane and hidden himself in the tail. No one had thought of the possibility of any person doing such an unthinking and dangerous thing. His action had added a weight at the start which might have thrown the plane out of the control of the most expert pilot. Assollant's feat of taking the overloaded, unbalanced ship off the sands was one of the most skillful maneuvers ever executed by any pilot. If it had crashed in all probability the entire crew would have been killed. In any case the plane would have been wrecked and the efforts of a year, time and money wasted.

Steadily the *Yellow Bird* roared on. Lefevre laid out a new course. Assollant headed the plane for the Azores. Fortunately the weather held fair and the night passed without unusual incident. One ship was sighted, and wirelessed the passage of the *Yellow Bird*. The gas dwindled and enabled them to climb to better flying levels. As morning came their hopes rose. They shared what little food they had with the stowaway. After their first justifiable anger they treated him with every consideration.

"Since he is here," Lotti said, "he is sharing our danger. He shall also share our food."

They altered their course again. The morning turned cloudy. Great masses of white cloud rolled down upon the *Yellow Bird*. They did not want the difficulty of flying blind through these huge soft mountains, so they flew over and around. But this took valuable gallons of gas. Afternoon brought darker clouds, treacherous winds, bumpy air and storm. They passed the Azores and kept in toward the coast of Spain.

Lotti examined the gasoline gauge.

"We can't reach Paris," he said. "We'll try to land on French soil."

They were nearing the end of the flight. Gallon by gallon the gasoline poured into the hungry motor. The coast of Spain rose before them. Twilight was falling and the sea below looked green and silver. Dim upon the skyline, the gaunt, brown, barren mountains of Spain lifted, scarcely darker than the clouds that had delayed them.

"Land wherever you can," Lotti said.

Assollant nodded in agreement. The last tank was almost empty. Looking down they saw the flat houses of a fishing village, boats at anchor on the quiet water, and a long shining empty beach.

Assollant pointed to the sand.

" Good, if it's hard enough," he said.

Down came the *Yellow Bird,* its propeller spinning idly. Lightly the wheels touched. The sand was as hard as concrete. The *Yellow Bird* rolled to a stop. From the village came dark-faced fishermen, their wives and children to see the great plane that had dropped from the evening skies onto this remote spot.

The three Frenchmen climbed out of the cabin. They had failed to reach their objective, but it had been no fault of theirs. They accepted the defeat with the same graciousness and sportsmanship with which they had accepted the presence of the stowaway. At least they were the first flyers of their nation to cross the North Atlantic and their names could be written beside those other great French pilots who bore honorable places on the records of aviation.

Shortly after the successful crossing of the Atlantic by the *Yellow Bird,* Williams and Yancey procured a new plane. They christened it the *Pathfinder* and made their sixth attempt to fly to Rome. This time their perseverance was partially rewarded. More care than ever was exercised on the take off to prevent a repetition of the disaster that had destroyed the *Green Flash.* The *Pathfinder* lifted easily from the hard beach at Old Orchard and accompanied by four planes, gradually swung east and began the hazardous voyage, following the southern route. Flying conditions were moderately bad and they were forced to waste gasoline in avoiding local storms. Beyond the Azores, gales and strong head winds set in. All their skill was needed to cross the remaining distance, and after a brilliant passage they reached Spain and made a landing a few miles beyond the point where the French crew came to earth. The next day they took off for Rome and completed the journey in ten hours of tranquil voyaging.

CONCLUSION

S CARCELY the first page of the story of flying has been written. From the fable of Icarus to the ascents of the hot-air balloons of the Montgolfier brothers is, if the legendary time of the Greek hero can be estimated—perhaps 2500 or 3000 years. Only 120 years had passed from the triumphal ascents of Jean and Jacques Montgolfier in their elaborate balloons, until Santos Dumont steered his unruly dirigible with its tiny sputtering engine about the Eiffel Tower. Still swifter is the progress of the airplane, from the three-second flight of the Wright Brothers at Kitty Hawk in 1903 to the 420 hours aloft of two young men in a cabin commercial monoplane in 1929 during which time they flew more than the distance around the world.

So much is happening, with such rapidity that no attempt has been made in this book to record more than a few of these astounding events. No mention has been made of such courageous accomplishments as the Army Round the World flyers, the Good Will flight to South America, the amazing circling of the globe by Brock and Schlee in the *Pride of Detroit,* or Lindbergh's flight of 2400 miles to Mexico.

Neither has any account been given of aviators in other countries; men of daring and vision; the English flyers, Capt. Ross Smith and his comrades voyaged from London to Australia; the flight from Cairo to Cape Town; the Australian Bert

Hinkler's long solo flight, the Frenchmen Costes and Lebrix; Girier and Dordilly who flew from Paris to Omsk, Siberia; Palletier D'Oisy on the flight from Paris to Peking, and Costes and Rignet who journeyed from Paris to Persia; the Italians, De Pinedo, Ferrarin and Del Prete; the Portuguese, Cabral and Coutinhs who first crossed the South Atlantic. Even this list does not include the journey of the *Norge* over the Pole, or the *Italia* disaster and the heroic exploits of Swedish, Norwegian, Italian and Russian pilots.

The next few years we may expect even more startling developments in the air. The refueling endurance flights of the *Question Mark,* the *Fort Worth* and the *Angeleno* have opened the possibility of an airplane circling the world without coming to rest. The Autogiro indicates a new type of machine, requiring little space for landing or taking off and an advancement in safety of air travel. A German flying-boat is being tested and will carry one hundred passengers and fly a regular route to South America. A plane has flown with a Deisel motor using fuel-oil instead of gasoline.

The air is filled with the drone of motors. Through the night the riding lights of the air mail flash like some new, strange star. On flying fields all over the world students await, hand on stick, the signal for their solo flights. Riders of the winds! Living the greatest of man's dreams.

————————

The author wishes to acknowledge his indebtedness for certain data to the following books and authors: *The Three Musketeers of the Air* by Koehl, Fitzmaurice and Huenefeld; *Flying the Arctic* by George Wilkins; *Historic Airships* by Rupert Sargent Holland; *The Flight of the Southern Cross* by C. E. Kingsford-Smith and C. P. Ulm; *Skyward* by Commander Richard E. Byrd; *20 Hours, 40 Minutes* by Amelia Earhart; *Conquering the Air* by Archibald Williams; *Heroes of the Air* by Chelsea Fraser; and *The Boys' Book of Airmen* by Irving Crump.